Summary of Contents

JUMP START BOOTSTRAP

BY SYED FAZLE RAHMAN

Jump Start Bootstrap

by Syed Fazle Rahman

Copyright © 2014 SitePoint Pty. Ltd.

Product Manager: Simon Mackie   **English Editor**: Kelly Steele

Technical Editor: Ivaylo Gerchev   **Cover Designer**: Alex Walker

Published by SitePoint Pty. Ltd.

48 Cambridge Street Collingwood
VIC Australia 3066
Web: www.sitepoint.com
Email: business@sitepoint.com

ISBN 978-0-9922794-3-1 (print)

ISBN 978-0-9922794-7-9 (ebook)
Printed and bound in the United States of America

About Syed Fazle Rahman

Syed Fazle Rahman is a web developer and a blogger, with over four years of freelancing experience. His expertise includes HTML5, CSS3, Less, JavaScript, jQuery, and Ember.js. He's currently working on hybrid applications for smartphones and smart TVs.

About SitePoint

SitePoint specializes in publishing fun, practical, and easy-to-understand content for web professionals. Visit http://www.sitepoint.com/ to access our blogs, books, newsletters, articles, and community forums. You'll find a stack of information on JavaScript, PHP, Ruby, mobile development, design, and more.

About Jump Start

Jump Start books provide you with a rapid and practical introduction to web development languages and technologies. Typically around 150 pages in length, they can be read in a weekend, giving you a solid grounding in the topic and the confidence to experiment on your own.

To my lovely parents, troublesome brother, cute sister, and my best buddy, Sandeep.

Table of Contents

Chapter 3   Exploring Bootstrap Components

Chapter 4 **Bootstrap Plugins for Fun and Profit** 89

Preface

Crafting a modern, professional website from scratch takes a lot of time and effort. Sites today need to be responsive, mobile first, slickly designed, and fast. Bootstrap helps designers and developers by providing a vast array of HTML components and a grid system that make creating professional, responsive templates a snap, and can greatly cut down development time.

Bootstrap is useful for everyone, but it's a blessing for novice developers. All the intricate CSS and JavaScript required to create complex web components are pre-written. Only some HTML markup is needed to make them work. More experienced developers can take advantage of the number of customization options that Bootstrap offers, including Less and Sass support.

Throughout this book, I have tried to provide a complete guide to the Bootstrap framework. We'll cover how we can build beautiful responsive websites without needing to gain expertise in advanced web development techniques. We'll discuss the various useful CSS components and JavaScript plugins that Bootstrap provides out of the box. We'll also cover various ways of customizing the look and feel of Bootstrap to generate completely unique designs.

Hopefully by now that you're excited to start building your first websites using the Bootstrap framework. By the end of this book, I am confident that you will have the skills to quickly create a beautiful responsive website template. I hope both this book, and the Bootstrap framework, satisfy your web designing needs.

Who Should Read This Book

This book is suitable for beginner to intermediate level web designers and developers. Experience of HTML and CSS is assumed, and some knowledge of JavaScript is helpful.

Conventions Used

You'll notice that we've used certain typographic and layout styles throughout this book to signify different types of information. Look out for the following items.

Code Samples

Code in this book will be displayed using a fixed-width font, like so:

```
<h1>A Perfect Summer's Day</h1>
<p>It was a lovely day for a walk in the park. The birds
were singing and the kids were all back at school.</p>
```

If the code is to be found in the book's code archive, the name of the file will appear at the top of the program listing, like this:

```
                                                        example.css
.footer {
  background-color: #CCC;
  border-top: 1px solid #333;
}
```

If only part of the file is displayed, this is indicated by the word *excerpt*:

```
                                              example.css (excerpt)
  border-top: 1px solid #333;
```

If additional code is to be inserted into an existing example, the new code will be displayed in bold:

```
function animate() {
  new_variable = "Hello";
}
```

Also, where existing code is required for context, rather than repeat all it, a ⋮ will be displayed:

```
function animate() {
  ⋮
  return new_variable;
}
```

Some lines of code are intended to be entered on one line, but we've had to wrap them because of page constraints. A ➡ indicates a line break that exists for formatting purposes only, and that should be ignored.

```
URL.open("http://www.sitepoint.com/responsive-web-design-real-user-
➡testing/?responsive1");
```

Tips, Notes, and Warnings

Hey, You!

Tips will give you helpful little pointers.

Ahem, Excuse Me ...

Notes are useful asides that are related—but not critical—to the topic at hand. Think of them as extra tidbits of information.

Make Sure You Always ...

... pay attention to these important points.

Watch Out!

Warnings will highlight any gotchas that are likely to trip you up along the way.

Supplementary Materials

http://www.sitepoint.com/store/jump-start-bootstrap/
The book's website, containing links, updates, resources, and more.

https://github.com/spbooks/jsbootstrap1
The downloadable code archive for this book.

http://www.sitepoint.com/forums/forumdisplay.php?53-CSS-amp-Page-Layout
SitePoint's forums, for help on any tricky web problems.

books@sitepoint.com

Our email address, should you need to contact us for support, to report a problem, or for any other reason.

Want to Take Your Learning Further?

Thanks for buying this book. We appreciate your support. Do you want to continue learning? You can now get unlimited access to courses and ALL SitePoint books at Learnable for one low price. Enroll now and start learning today! Join Learnable and you'll stay ahead of the newest technology trends: http://www.learnable.com.

Up, Close, and Personal with Bootstrap

In this chapter, we'll learn the basics of Bootstrap and understand how it can speed up the web development process. We'll start with a brief overview of the history of CSS frameworks and then move on to explain the term **Responsive Web Design**, or RWD. Finally, we'll see how to set up a new Bootstrap project and use it to create our first basic web page.

What is Bootstrap?

Bootstrap is a front-end framework that helps developers to jump start the web development process. Developers who are moving to front-end development from hardcore server-side programming languages such as Java or PHP can find it very difficult to come to grips with CSS and JavaScript; however, with Bootstrap they only have to concentrate on writing proper HTML, leaving the tricky CSS and JavaScript to Bootstrap.

Bootstrap is not only useful for novice web developers. As we proceed throughout the book, you will come to see how Bootstrap can be a boon for expert coders too.

Why Does It Exist?

Imagine you have to design a website with an attractive navigation bar, stylish buttons, nice typography, placeholders for texts and images, a big image slider, and more—yet you aren't a front end development expert. But what if these features were already coded for you, and you just had to write a little HTML to use them? This is Bootstrap.

All the CSS classes and JavaScript code needed are already included in the Bootstrap package. For example, using the class btn with link (<a></a>) elements will make them appear like a button as seen in Figure 1.1. Additionally, using the btn-primary class with a link will make it a dark blue button:

```
<a href="http://www.google.com" class="btn btn-primary">
➦Visit Google</a>
```

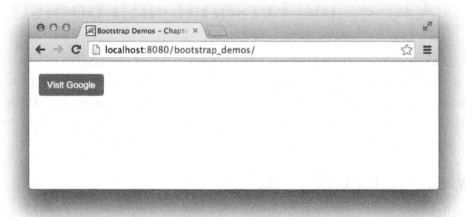

Figure 1.1. Creating a button with Bootstrap

Yet Bootstrap is more than just decorating links, images and typography. One of its most important features is the **grid system**. You cannot create a mobile-friendly and responsive website without the grid system. We'll discuss responsive web design and the grid system later in this chapter.

How Can It Help Me?

As I've mentioned, Bootstrap is a plus for a novice designer, but it's not restricted to novices. Experts can also use Bootstrap's code as a base to create something new. Bootstrap allows you to customize its styles through the use of Less[1] and Sass[2]. Developers acquainted with these technologies can completely modify Bootstrap's default look and feel. There are multiple ways of customizing Bootstrap, and we'll look at these in a later chapter.

History of CSS Frameworks

It all started when CSS frameworks like YUI[3] (Yahoo User Interface Library) and Blueprint[4] became popular around 2006-07. They brought with them many fundamental resources like CSS reset, fonts, grids, animation effects, buttons, and so on. Developers began to realize that these frameworks were useful for dealing with many of the tedious repetitive tasks required to develop a website, and that their use could greatly improve development turnaround time.

These basic CSS frameworks were followed by a generation of "full fledged" front-end frameworks, such as Bootstrap, which added JavaScript to the mix. Bootstrap combined commonly used CSS and JavaScript components together, catering to many basic development requirements, such as creating sliders, making pop-up effects, and drop-down menus.

Bootstrap encapsulates many useful components that can be easily employed in website projects. It uses standard HTML markup for each component. With Bootstrap, developers have only to focus on writing proper HTML markup that the framework can understand and render accordingly.

The Need for CSS Prototyping

The main reason for having a good CSS framework is to ease the development process. There are many common tasks that every web designer caries out while developing a website. Tasks such as clearing browser resets, creating a proper grid system

---

[1] http://lesscss.org/
[2] http://sass-lang.com/
[3] http://yuilibrary.com/
[4] http://www.blueprintcss.org/

for website layout, and assigning typography rules can become frustrating and time-consuming if done repeatedly for every project. A good CSS framework provides a powerful set of tools that streamline these tasks.

Some of the main highlights of a good CSS framework include:

- faster development
- organized and maintainable code
- allowing you to spend time on innovation rather than reinventing the wheel.

The Origins of Bootstrap

Bootstrap was developed in 2011 by Mark Otto and Jacob Thornton, a pair of web developers at Twitter. Their main focus was to bring consistency and maintainability in their code.

Here's a quote from Mark Otto's blog[5] about the genesis of Bootstrap:

> ... [A] super small group of developers and I got together to design and build a new internal tool and saw an opportunity to do something more. Through that process, we saw ourselves build something much more substantial than another internal tool. Months later, we ended up with an early version of Bootstrap as a way to document and share common design patterns and assets within the company.

Bootstrap 1.0.0 was launched in 2011 with only CSS and HTML components. There were no JavaScript plugins included in it until Bootstrap 1.3.0, a version that was also compatible with IE7 and IE8.

2012 saw another major update with Bootstrap 2.0.0. It was a complete rewrite of the Bootstrap library, as well as becoming a responsive framework. Its components were compatible with all kinds of devices—mobiles, tablets and desktops—and lots of new CSS and JavaScript plugins were included in the package.

After 15 major updates, Bootstrap 3 in 2013 was another significant release, becoming a "Mobile First and always responsive" framework. In the earlier versions of the framework, making a responsive website was optional. In the 2013 release, there were changes in the names of the classes and also in the folder structure of the

---

[5] http://markdotto.com/

project. Be aware, though, that **Bootstrap 3 is not backward compatible**. You cannot directly migrate to this version by replacing the core CSS and JavaScript files.

If you want to have a look at the complete journey of Bootstrap, check out historical releases on GitHub.[6] It also shows the changes that were made to each version.

Today, Bootstrap has a huge global community of developers who regularly contribute to its code base at GitHub. It also has an active discussion at the Stack Overflow community with tags such as bootstrap[7], twitter-bootstrap[8] and twitter-bootstrap-3[9].

Bootstrap has become one of the most sought after technologies today. It is a must-have if you are a full-stack developer, as show by the screenshot in Figure 1.2 from Indeed.com's Bootstrap job trends.

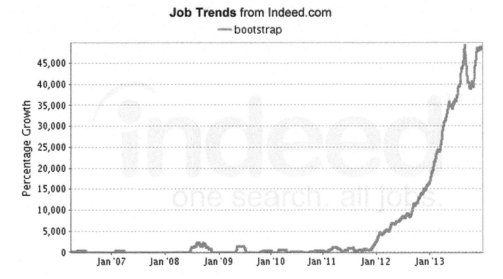

Figure 1.2. Bootstrap skills in demand

---

[6] https://github.com/twbs/bootstrap/releases

[7] http://stackoverflow.com/questions/tagged/bootstrap

[8] http://stackoverflow.com/questions/tagged/twitter-bootstrap

[9] http://stackoverflow.com/questions/tagged/twitter-bootstrap-3

At the time of writing, Bootstrap 3.1.1 is the latest version. Hence, the book's content and code will be compatible with Bootstrap 3.1.1 and above.

Bootstrap's Competition

There are many other popular frameworks that are competing with Bootstrap in the front-end framework arena. Some of them are:

- Foundation framework by Zurb[10]
- Semantic UI[11]
- Gumby framework[12]
- Pure by Yahoo[13]

Who Uses Bootstrap?

It's worthwhile checking out real-life projects based on a technology before adopting it. It can help to give a clear understanding of what can be achieved using that particular technology. Here are some examples of real-life website projects that have been created with the help of Bootstrap:

- OpenDesk[14]
- Riot Designs[15]
- 20Jeans[16]
- Red Antler[17]
- Uberflip[18]

---

[10] http://foundation.zurb.com/
[11] http://semantic-ui.com/
[12] http://gumbyframework.com/
[13] http://purecss.io/
[14] https://www.opendesk.cc/
[15] http://riotdesign.eu/en/
[16] https://www.20jeans.com/
[17] http://redantler.com/
[18] www.uberflip.com

Overview of Responsive Web Design

Responsive web design allows developers to create a website that can change its layout on the go. Developers can then create a single design that works on any kind of device: mobiles, tablets, smart TVs, and PCs.

Sites designed responsively are generally fluid designs. They readjust themselves according to the size of the screen they are viewed in and are also compatible with the touch interfaces of mobile devices. Using responsive web design, developers can create powerful web apps that replace native apps on platforms such as iOS and Android.

Adjusting a Layout Based on Screen Size

Let's check out an example to better understand this concept. Suppose we have the layout shown in Figure 1.3 for a desktop screen.

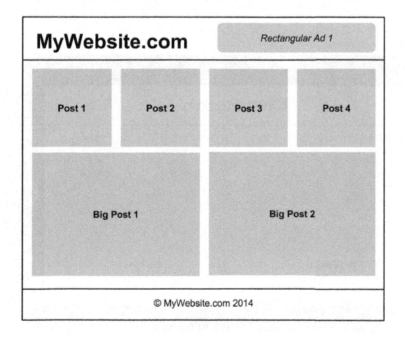

Figure 1.3. Our layout for a desktop screen

We have three main sections in our desktop layout: the header, the content section, and the footer area. The header section contains a logo and a rectangular ad. The content section contains four smaller posts placed side by side horizontally. We then have two bigger posts placed underneath the smaller posts. Finally, we have a footer section in which there is simple copyright text.

It is obvious that we're unable to easily view this page on our tablets and cell phones as it will fail to fit the screen properly. The design needs to be customized for those users.

Let's suppose we have used Bootstrap to create the desktop layout. We have used its grid system to create a responsive design so that the layout will automatically adjust to suit tablets and mobile devices.

On tablet devices, the layout will appear as shown in Figure 1.4. The ad has been hidden from the header section and the logo has been centered. The layout fits perfectly.

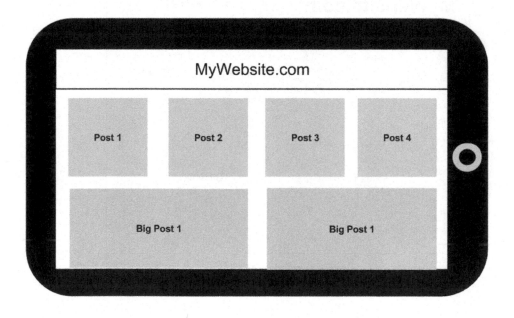

Figure 1.4. Our layout adjusted for tablet screens

In the smartphone view, shown in Figure 1.5, we can see that the header section continues to follow the tablet view but there's a major change in the content section. The posts reflow themselves to the bottom forming two rows, each containing two posts. The bigger posts are now placed on top of each other—one post in one row (the second big post is off the bottom of the screen).

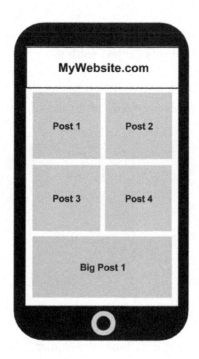

Figure 1.5. Our layout adjusted for smartphones

That's a very basic overview of how a responsive design behaves. We can obviously do a lot more than what is shown in the aforementioned example. We'll learn more about responsive web design while studying grid systems in Chapter 2.

Getting Bootstrap Ready

Finally we have arrived at the most important topic in this chapter: getting our hands dirty with Bootstrap!

First we need the Bootstrap package, so let's go to the official Bootstrap website at http://getbootstrap.com and download the latest 3.x.x version. Extract the archive file and copy the following folders:

```
- /css
- /fonts
- /js
```

Create a project folder with any name you wish. I have named mine **Bootstrap_demos**. Paste the above folders into this project folder.

Now open up your favorite HTML editor (I personally recommend Sublime Text[19]), create a new file called **index.html**, and enter the following code snippet into it:

```html
<!DOCTYPE html>
<html lang="en">
  <head>
    <title>My First Bootstrap Application</title>
  </head>
  <body>

  </body>
</html>
```

This is a simple HTML structure for our first Bootstrap app.

Our project directory should now look like Figure 1.6.

---

[19] http://www.sublimetext.com/

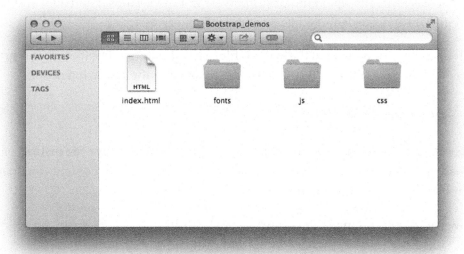

Figure 1.6. Our initial project folder structure

Now let's include Bootstrap inside our HTML file. First, we need to include Bootstrap's CSS file. Open up the **/css** folder and you should see a file named **bootstrap.css**. This is Bootstrap's main CSS file.

What's bootstrap.min.css?

There's also another file named **bootstrap.min.css**, which is the **minified** version of **bootstrap.css**. It is called minified because it has no spaces and no comments, which reduces the size of the file. It will be used when your project is completed and is ready for production.

Let's link our CSS file into **index.html**. Place the following inside the `<head>` tag and below the `<title>` tag:

```
<link rel="stylesheet" type="text/css" href="css/bootstrap.css">
```

Bootstrap requires jQuery for its JavaScript components to work. Go to jquery.com[20] and download jQuery version 1.11.0. Bootstrap supports Internet Explorer 8 and above. If you download jQuery version 2, IE8+ will fail to function properly because

---

[20] http://jquery.com/

jQuery has officially opted out of support for IE8 in versions 2 and above. Hence, jQuery 1.11.0 is needed, the latest version of jQuery 1.

After you have downloaded the **jquery.js** file, paste it into the **/js** folder of your project directory. Next, we'll link it into our **index.html** using the following code:

```
<script src="js/jquery.js"></script>
```

It is recommended that you insert jQuery just inside the <body> tag instead of the <head> tag. This is so that jQuery is loaded after all the HTML contents are loaded, reducing the page's loading time.

Now we have to include Bootstrap's JavaScript file:

```
<script src="js/bootstrap.js"></script>
```

index.html should now look like this:

```
<!DOCTYPE html>
<html lang="en">
  <head>
    <title>My First Bootstrap Application</title>
    <link rel="stylesheet" type="text/css" href="css/bootstrap.css">
  </head>
  <body>

        <script src="js/jquery.js"></script>
        <script src="js/bootstrap.js"></script>
  </body>
</html>
```

In order to make Bootstrap completely compatible with every kind of device, we need to include some necessary meta tags.

First, we should tell browsers that our website contains characters from the Unicode character set, a superset of the ASCII character set. This is done using the following meta tag:

```
<meta charset="utf-8">
```

Sometimes, Internet Explorer may run in **compatibility mode**. Using the following code snippet would force IE to use the latest rendering engine to render our website. This will prevent our website from breaking as older rendering engines do not support all properties of CSS:

```
<meta http-equiv="X-UA-Compatible" content="IE=edge">
```

Next, we'll make our site consume all the space available inside the browser window, whether it's a tablet or a mobile or even a desktop screen. We tell the browser to scale our application to the size of window space available:

```
<meta name="viewport" content="width=device-width, initial-scale=1">
```

initial-scale=1 in the code means scale it to 100%.

Now our **index.html** should look like this:

```
<!DOCTYPE html>
<html lang="en">
  <head>
    <meta charset="utf-8">
    <meta http-equiv="X-UA-Compatible" content="IE=edge">
    <meta name="viewport" content="width=device-width,
➥initial-scale=1">

    <title>My First Bootstrap Application</title>
    <link rel="stylesheet" type="text/css" href="css/bootstrap.css">
  </head>
  <body>

        <script src="js/jquery.js"></script>
        <script src="js/bootstrap.js"></script>
  </body>
</html>
```

There's one final step we need to deal with in the above code. Bootstrap 3 uses many HTML5 elements and CSS3 properties that won't work in Internet Explorer 8. We now have to add some scripts that will only be called into action when the website is opened in IE8, bringing support for HTML5 and CSS3 in it. These scripts are **html5shiv.js** and **respond.js**:

```
<!--[if lt IE 9]>
    <script src="https://oss.maxcdn.com/libs/html5shiv/
➡3.7.0/html5shiv.js"></script>
    <script src="https://oss.maxcdn.com/libs/respond.js/
➡1.4.2/respond.min.js"></script>
    <![endif]-->
```

Using These Scripts

You don't have to download **html5shiv.js** and **respond.js**. You can simply directly link to their CDN, as shown above.

Now our **index.html** page is complete. It should look like this:

```
<!DOCTYPE html>
<html lang="en">
  <head>
    <meta charset="utf-8">
    <meta http-equiv="X-UA-Compatible" content="IE=edge">
    <meta name="viewport" content="width=device-width,
➡initial-scale=1">

    <title>My First Bootstrap Application</title>
    <link rel="stylesheet" type="text/css" href="css/bootstrap.css">

    <!--[if lt IE 9]>
    <script src="https://oss.maxcdn.com/libs/html5shiv/
➡3.7.0/html5shiv.js"></script>
    <script src="https://oss.maxcdn.com/libs/
➡respond.js/1.4.2/respond.min.js"></script>
    <![endif]-->

  </head>
  <body>
        <h1>Hello World!</h1>

        <script src="js/jquery.js"></script>
```

```
        <script src="js/bootstrap.js"></script>
  </body>
</html>
```

I have included an h1 element containing "Hello World!". Go ahead and load the page in your browser. You should see "Hello World!" written in a nice font.

If you are using Google Chrome, you have an easy option to check that all the JavaScript and CSS files are loaded properly. Right-click on the page and go to **Inspect Element**. Click on the **Console** tab and if no errors are displayed, all the JavaScript files have loaded properly. Next, go to the **Network** tab; if there are no 404 errors, all the CSS files are linked properly.

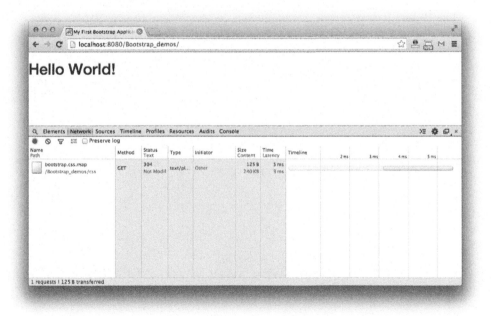

Figure 1.7. Checking that files have loaded correctly in Chrome

Finally, we are done with setting up our Bootstrap project. We'll be using a similar set up in the rest of this book.

Bootstrap Grid System

In this chapter, we'll discover one of the most important features of Bootstrap: the **grid system**. We'll learn how the grid system works and how we can use it in our applications. We'll also create some sample website layouts in order to understand it better.

What Is a Grid System?

A **grid system** allows us to properly house our website's content. It divides the screen into multiple rows and columns that can be used to create various types of layouts. Once we have the rows and columns defined, we can decide which HTML element will be placed where.

Bootstrap's grid system divides the screen into columns—up to 12 in each row. The column widths vary according to the size of screen they're displayed in. Hence, Bootstrap's grid system is **responsive**, as the columns resize themselves dynamically when the size of browser window changes. You can create an infinite number of rows depending on your design's requirements. The intersection of these rows and columns forms a rectangular grid to contain the website's content.

As an example, in Figure 2.1 I have created a row and then used the grid system to divide it into 12 columns. I have changed each column's background color to make them distinct. Each column here is represented by a number.

Figure 2.1. A sample page showing a 12-column grid

Building a Basic Grid

In this section, we're going to create our first website layout using Bootstrap's grid system. We will be using the same Bootstrap setup, `Bootstrap_demos`, that we created in the last chapter. Copy all the files that are present inside the `Bootstrap_demos` folder. Then create a new folder called `chapter_2` and paste those files inside it.

Now open `index.html`, change the page title to "Bootstrap Grid System" and remove the `<h1>` tag from the body. We should now have a basic HTML page that looks like this:

```
<!DOCTYPE html>
<html lang="en">
  <head>
    <meta charset="utf-8">
    <meta http-equiv="X-UA-Compatible" content="IE=edge">
    <meta name="viewport" content="width=device-width,
➥initial-scale=1">

    <title>Bootstrap Grid System</title>
    <link rel="stylesheet" type="text/css" href="css/bootstrap.css">
```

```
    <!--[if lt IE 9]>
      <script src="https://oss.maxcdn.com/libs/html5shiv/
➥3.7.0/html5shiv.js"></script>
      <script src="https://oss.maxcdn.com/libs/respond.js/
➥1.4.2/respond.min.js"></script>
    <![endif]-->

  </head>
  <body>
      <!-- Body content goes here -->

      <script src="js/jquery.js"></script>
      <script src="js/bootstrap.js"></script>
  </body>
</html>
```

Bootstrap recommends that we should place all the rows and columns inside a container to ensure proper alignment and padding. There are two types of container classes in Bootstrap: `container` and `container-fluid`. The former creates a fixed-width container in the browser window, while the latter creates a full-width fluid container. The fixed-width container is styled to appear at the center of the screen, omitting extra space on both sides. Hence, it is a good practice to wrap all the contents within a container.

We will use the fixed-width `container` in our demo. Let's go ahead and create a container in our HTML page:

```
<div class="container">
</div>
```

Next, we'll create a row inside a container. Once the row is defined, we can start creating the columns. Bootstrap has a class `row` for creating rows:

```
<div class="container">
    <div class="row">
    </div>
</div>
```

You can create an infinite number of rows but they must be placed within a container. For better results, it is recommended to have a single container with all the rows inside it.

In Bootstrap, columns are created by specifying how many of the 12 available Bootstrap columns you wish to span. Suppose we want to have only a single column. It should span across all twelve available Bootstrap columns. For this we'll use the class col-xs-12, with the number 12 specifying the amount of columns to span. (You can ignore the xs term in the class name for now; we'll discuss that later).

Similarly, to create two equal-width columns in a row, we'd use the class col-xs-6 for each one. This tells Bootstrap that we want two columns that span across six of Bootstrap's columns, as follows:

```
<div class="container">
    <div class="row">
        <div class="col-xs-6">
            <h4>Column 1</h4>
        </div>
        <div class="col-xs-6">
            <h4>Column 2</h4>
        </div>
    </div>
</div>
```

The result can be seen in Figure 2.2.

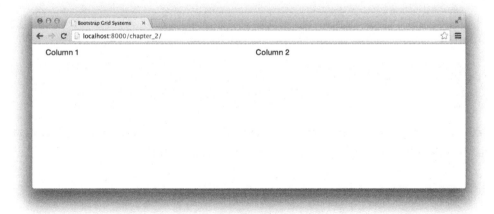

Figure 2.2. Two equally sized columns on our grid

To make our columns clearer, let's give each one a background color. We'll create a new CSS file called **styles.css** inside the CSS folder of our project. It's not a standard filename, you can name it anything you wish. Next, we'll link this file in our **index.html** using a `link` element inside the `head` element:

```
<link href="css/styles.css" rel="stylesheet">
```

Let's drop some CSS into this file to make each column have a different background color:

```
.col1{
    background: #5C7080;
}

.col2{
    background: #6BC0FF;
}
```

We also have to add the classes `col1` and `col2` in our markup so that the columns pick their respective CSS styling. The updated markup is as follows:

```
<div class="container">
    <div class="row">
        <div class="col-xs-6 col1">
            <h4>Column 1</h4>
        </div>
        <div class="col-xs-6 col2">
            <h4>Column 2</h4>
```

```
            </div>
        </div>
    </div>
```

Figure 2.3. A two-column layout with background color styling

But what does the `xs` stand for in the class `col-xs-6`? Bootstrap has four types of class prefixes for creating columns for different size displays:

1. `col-xs` for extra small displays (screen width < 768px)
2. `col-sm` for smaller displays (screen width ≥ 768px)
3. `col-md` for medium displays (screen width ≥ 992px)
4. `col-lg` for larger displays (screen width ≥ 1200px)

When we specify the class `col-xs-12`, it means the element should span all 12 of the available Bootstrap columns on extra small screens. But what about larger displays? In the above code, we haven't specified how the div should behave on larger screen types. Fortunately, Bootstrap will automatically follow the layout specified for the smallest screen size. Hence, our div will span 12 columns in all types of displays in this code.

Let's examine the following markup:

```
<div class="container">
    <div class="row">
        <div class="col-xs-12 col-sm-6 col1">
```

```
            <h4>Column 1</h4>
        </div>
        <div class="col-xs-12 col-sm-6 col2">
            <h4>Column 2</h4>
        </div>
    </div>
</div>
```

In this code we have used the class col-xs-12 for an extra small display and class col-sm-6 for a smaller sized display. Hence, each column in an extra small-sized display will occupy all the 12 available Bootstrap columns, which will appear as a stack of columns. Yet on a smaller display, they will occupy only six Bootstrap columns each to achieve a two-column layout as shown in Figure 2.4. .

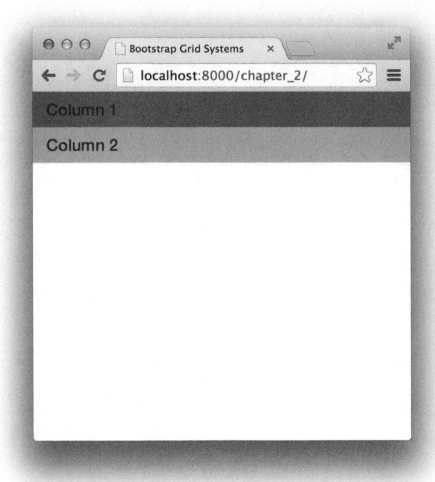

Figure 2.4. The layout on smaller screens

Let's add another row of columns in the previous code. We'll replicate the same markup that was used to create a row in the code. The final markup for two rows and four columns in our layout is as follows:

```
<div class="container">
    <div class="row">
        <div class="col-xs-12 col-sm-6 col1">
            <h4>Column 1</h4>
        </div>
```

```
        <div class="col-xs-12 col-sm-6 col2">
            <h4>Column 2</h4>
        </div>
    </div>
    <div class="row">
        <div class="col-xs-12 col-sm-6 col3">
            <h4>Column 3</h4>
        </div>
        <div class="col-xs-12 col-sm-6 col4">
            <h4>Column 4</h4>
        </div>
    </div>
</div>
```

I have added two new classes, col3 and col4, to give our columns different background colors:

```
.col3{
    background: #E8AA4C;
}

.col4{
    background: #FF384E;
}
```

And here's the result, shown in Figure 2.5.

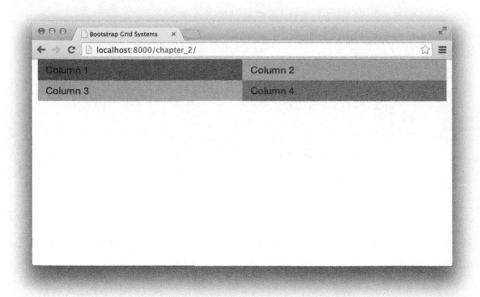

Figure 2.5. A two-row, four-column layout

Case Study: Creating a Dynamic Layout

Let's see how to put the grid system into practice, creating a dynamic layout that adjusts to the size of device it is viewed in.

Suppose we have to create a blog layout using the Bootstrap framework. We're given the wireframe shown in Figure 2.6 for the desktop display.

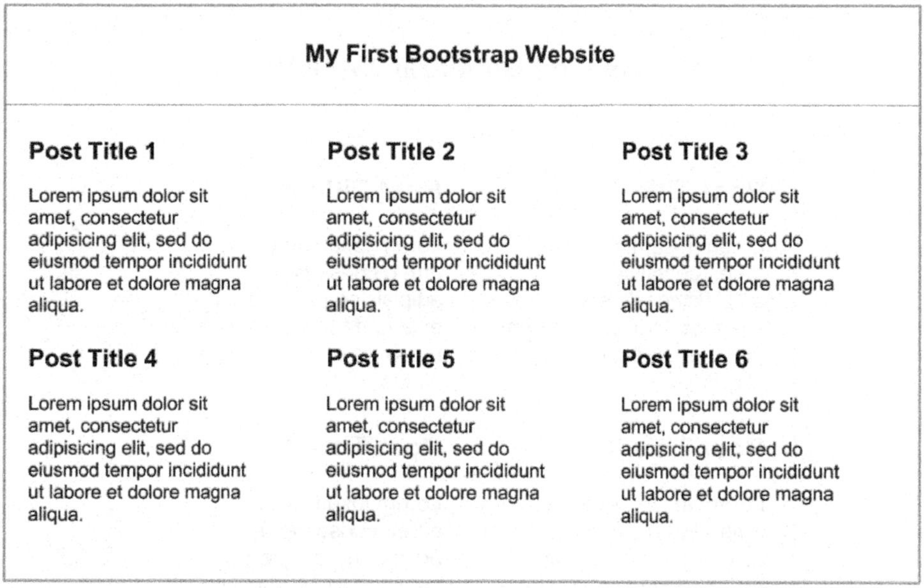

My First Bootstrap Website

Post Title 1

Lorem ipsum dolor sit amet, consectetur adipisicing elit, sed do eiusmod tempor incididunt ut labore et dolore magna aliqua.

Post Title 2

Lorem ipsum dolor sit amet, consectetur adipisicing elit, sed do eiusmod tempor incididunt ut labore et dolore magna aliqua.

Post Title 3

Lorem ipsum dolor sit amet, consectetur adipisicing elit, sed do eiusmod tempor incididunt ut labore et dolore magna aliqua.

Post Title 4

Lorem ipsum dolor sit amet, consectetur adipisicing elit, sed do eiusmod tempor incididunt ut labore et dolore magna aliqua.

Post Title 5

Lorem ipsum dolor sit amet, consectetur adipisicing elit, sed do eiusmod tempor incididunt ut labore et dolore magna aliqua.

Post Title 6

Lorem ipsum dolor sit amet, consectetur adipisicing elit, sed do eiusmod tempor incididunt ut labore et dolore magna aliqua.

Figure 2.6. A wireframe of the site as it should appear on desktop displays

In the wireframe, we have a header that spans across the width of the whole website. Then we have a three-column layout containing blog posts. If we view the same layout in a tablet (portrait mode), it will look very clumsy. Hence, we have a re-designed the wireframe for tablet mode, as shown in Figure 2.7.

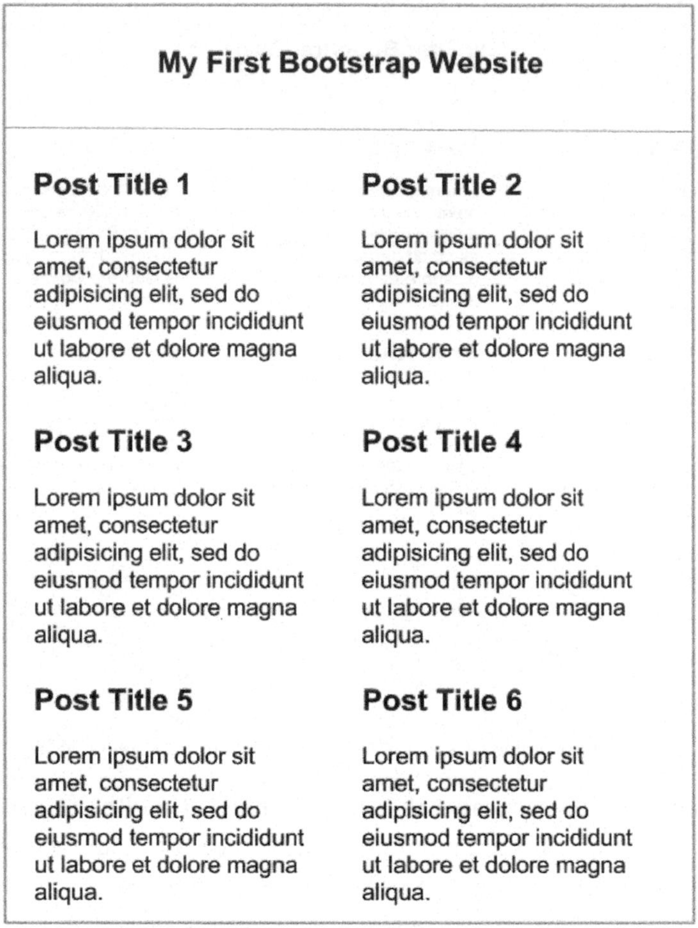

My First Bootstrap Website

Post Title 1

Lorem ipsum dolor sit amet, consectetur adipisicing elit, sed do eiusmod tempor incididunt ut labore et dolore magna aliqua.

Post Title 2

Lorem ipsum dolor sit amet, consectetur adipisicing elit, sed do eiusmod tempor incididunt ut labore et dolore magna aliqua.

Post Title 3

Lorem ipsum dolor sit amet, consectetur adipisicing elit, sed do eiusmod tempor incididunt ut labore et dolore magna aliqua.

Post Title 4

Lorem ipsum dolor sit amet, consectetur adipisicing elit, sed do eiusmod tempor incididunt ut labore et dolore magna aliqua.

Post Title 5

Lorem ipsum dolor sit amet, consectetur adipisicing elit, sed do eiusmod tempor incididunt ut labore et dolore magna aliqua.

Post Title 6

Lorem ipsum dolor sit amet, consectetur adipisicing elit, sed do eiusmod tempor incididunt ut labore et dolore magna aliqua.

Figure 2.7. A wireframe of the site as it should appear on tablet displays

In this design, we see that the header looks the same as in desktop mode. The posts underneath are now contained in a two-column layout instead of three. Next, we'll need to view the same website on mobile devices. The wireframe for a mobile display is shown in Figure 2.8.

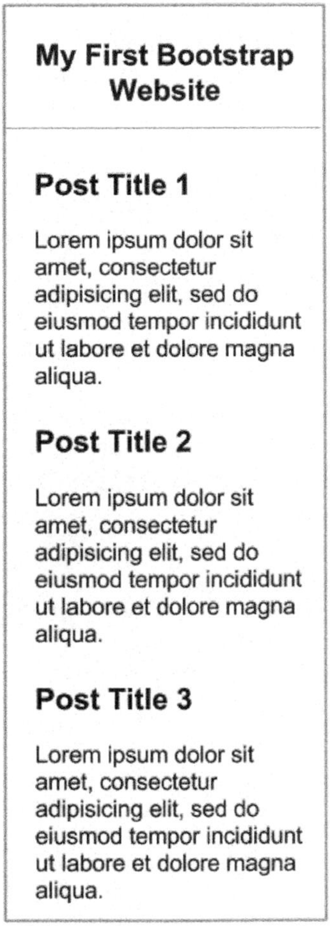

My First Bootstrap Website

Post Title 1

Lorem ipsum dolor sit amet, consectetur adipisicing elit, sed do eiusmod tempor incididunt ut labore et dolore magna aliqua.

Post Title 2

Lorem ipsum dolor sit amet, consectetur adipisicing elit, sed do eiusmod tempor incididunt ut labore et dolore magna aliqua.

Post Title 3

Lorem ipsum dolor sit amet, consectetur adipisicing elit, sed do eiusmod tempor incididunt ut labore et dolore magna aliqua.

Figure 2.8. A wireframe of the site as it should appear on mobile displays

We have just converted the two columns into one column in a mobile design.

Let's discuss how to achieve this design in our markup.

Designing for Desktops

As stated, medium-sized displays are considered larger than 992px. Desktop displays are mostly larger than this size. Thus, we will be using the class with prefix `col-md` to lay out the columns in desktop displays. This layout will also be followed in larger displays that are larger than 1200px, so for this design we can ignore adding classes with prefix `col-lg` as they'd have no additional effect on the layout.

Create a new HTML file called **blog.html**. Paste the basic HTML structure with Bootstrap set up, as stated in the previous chapter. Change the content of the `<title>` tag to "My First Bootstrap Website" and remove the `<h1>` tag from the body. The markup for **blog.html** should look like this:

```
<!DOCTYPE html>
    <html lang="en">
      <head>
        <meta charset="utf-8">
        <meta http-equiv="X-UA-Compatible" content="IE=edge">
        <meta name="viewport" content="width=device-width,
➥initial-scale=1">

        <title>My First Bootstrap Website</title>
        <link rel="stylesheet" type="text/css"
➥href="css/bootstrap.css">

        <!--[if lt IE 9]>
          <script src="https://oss.maxcdn.com/libs/html5shiv/
➥3.7.0/html5shiv.js"></script>
          <script src="https://oss.maxcdn.com/libs/respond.js/
➥1.4.2/respond.min.js"></script>
        <![endif]-->

      </head>
      <body>
          <!-- Body content goes here -->

          <script src="js/jquery.js"></script>
          <script src="js/bootstrap.js"></script>
      </body>
    </html>
```

We need to first make a container to hold all the blog's content. Let's go with a fixed-width container using the class `container`:

```
<div class="container">
</div>
```

Next, we have a header as per the desktop wireframe. Let's create a row with a single column that spans across all 12 Bootstrap columns.

```
<div class="container">
    <div class="row">
        <div class="col-md-12 text-center">
            <h1>My First Bootstrap Blog</h1>
        </div>
    </div>
</div>
```

In the above code, I've used Bootstrap's helper class `text-center` to align the text inside the column. We're now done with the header.

Now to create a three-column layout that will hold the blog posts. Since we have a total of 12 Bootstrap columns to use, we'll let our columns span across four Bootstrap columns each. This way we'll have three equally sized columns. Let's devise a new row and start building columns with the class `col-md-4`:

```
<div class="container">
    <div class="row">
        <div class="col-md-12 text-center">
            <h1>My First Bootstrap Blog</h1>
        </div>
    </div>

    <hr>

    <div class="row">
        <div class="col-md-4">

        </div>
        <div class="col-md-4">

        </div>
        <div class="col-md-4">

        </div>
    </div>
</div>
```

I have also used an <hr> in between two rows to draw a horizontal line after the header.

It's time to fill the columns with some dummy content. We'll use an <h3> tag and a <p> tag with some *lorem ipsum* text for this purpose:

```
<div class="container">
    <div class="row">
        <div class="col-md-12 text-center">
            <h1>My First Bootstrap Blog</h1>
        </div>
    </div>

    <hr>

    <div class="row">
        <div class="col-md-4">
            <h3>Post Title 1</h3>
            <p>Lorem ipsum dolor sit amet, consectetur adipisicing
➥elit, sed do eiusmod tempor incididunt ut labore et dolore magna
➥aliqua. </p>
        </div>
        <div class="col-md-4">
            <h3>Post Title 2</h3>
            <p>Lorem ipsum dolor sit amet, consectetur adipisicing
➥elit, sed do eiusmod tempor incididunt ut labore et dolore magna
➥aliqua. </p>
        </div>
        <div class="col-md-4">
            <h3>Post Title 3</h3>
            <p>Lorem ipsum dolor sit amet, consectetur adipisicing
➥elit, sed do eiusmod tempor incididunt ut labore et dolore magna
➥aliqua. </p>
        </div>
    </div>
</div>
```

The **blog.html** page will look like Figure 2.9.

Figure 2.9. Our incomplete blog layout on desktop displays

As per the wireframe for a desktop display, we're still left with another three columns of blog posts. This time, we won't create a separate row for the next three columns. Instead, we'll directly append these columns to the existing row of columns in the previous code. You might be wondering how we can have 24 columns (six columns spanning across four Bootstrap columns each) in just a single row. Well, Bootstrap allows only 12 Bootstrap columns in a single row. If we try to exceed that, the rest of the columns will be adjusted into the next line. This new line will again have the capacity of 12 Bootstrap columns. This way we can tie all the blog post columns into a single row.

Let's go ahead and update the markup with three new columns:

```
<div class="container">
    <div class="row">
        <div class="col-md-12 text-center">
            <h1>My First Bootstrap Blog</h1>
        </div>
    </div>

    <hr>

    <div class="row">
        <div class="col-md-4">
            <h3>Post Title 1</h3>
            <p>Lorem ipsum dolor sit amet ... </p>
        </div>
```

```
        <div class="col-md-4">
            <h3>Post Title 2</h3>
            <p>Lorem ipsum dolor sit amet ... </p>
        </div>
        <div class="col-md-4">
            <h3>Post Title 3</h3>
            <p>Lorem ipsum dolor sit amet ... </p>
        </div>
        <div class="col-md-4">
            <h3>Post Title 4</h3>
            <p>Lorem ipsum dolor sit amet ... </p>
        </div>
        <div class="col-md-4">
            <h3>Post Title 5</h3>
            <p>Lorem ipsum dolor sit amet ... </p>
        </div>
        <div class="col-md-4">
            <h3>Post Title 6</h3>
            <p>Lorem ipsum dolor sit amet ... </p>
        </div>
    </div>
</div>
```

Finally, we have converted the desktop wireframe into an HTML page as shown in Figure 2.10.

Figure 2.10. Our complete blog layout on desktop displays

Designing for Tablets

Let's now modify our code to achieve the wireframe layout for tablets. Unlike desktop displays, tablets can be viewed in two formats: **Portrait** and **Landscape**. A tablet's landscape view is considered a medium-sized display (**screen width ≥ 992px**), which we've already taken care of using col-md-* classes. We're now left with the portrait view, which is a small-sized display. This can be achieved using col-sm-* classes.

Since we have to achieve a two-column layout in smaller displays, we have to force each column to span across six Bootstrap columns. This way we get only two columns (two by six Bootstrap columns = 12 Bootstrap columns) in each row. But here we have only one row. Hence, once all the 12 Bootstrap columns are occupied, the remaining columns will appear in the next line creating a new row each time.

Let's proceed and add an extra class col-sm-6 to our desktop layout code:

```
<div class="container">
    <div class="row">
        <div class="col-md-12 text-center">
            <h1>My First Bootstrap Blog</h1>
        </div>
    </div>

    <hr>

    <div class="row">
        <div class="col-md-4 col-sm-6">
            <h3>Post Title 1</h3>
            <p>Lorem ipsum dolor sit amet ... </p>
        </div>
        <div class="col-md-4 col-sm-6">
            <h3>Post Title 2</h3>
            <p>Lorem ipsum dolor sit amet ... </p>
        </div>
        <div class="col-md-4 col-sm-6">
            <h3>Post Title 3</h3>
            <p>Lorem ipsum dolor sit amet ... </p>
        </div>
        <div class="col-md-4 col-sm-6">
            <h3>Post Title 4</h3>
            <p>Lorem ipsum dolor sit amet ... </p>
```

```
        </div>
        <div class="col-md-4 col-sm-6">
            <h3>Post Title 5</h3>
            <p>Lorem ipsum dolor sit amet ... </p>
        </div>
        <div class="col-md-4 col-sm-6">
            <h3>Post Title 6</h3>
            <p>Lorem ipsum dolor sit amet ... </p>
        </div>
    </div>
</div>
```

So, as shown in Figure 2.11, we have two layouts for tablets: a three-column layout for landscape mode and a two-column layout in portrait mode.

Figure 2.11. A two-column layout for tablets

Designing for Mobile

Like tablets, mobiles can also be viewed in landscape and portrait mode. In the case of most mobile phones, both Landscape and Portrait view is classed as an extra small-sized displays (*screen width < 768px*). For larger phones, sometimes called phablets, like the Samsung Galaxy Note 3 and Motorola Droid Razr HD, the landscape mode would be classed as a small-sized display.

As per the wireframe for a mobile device, we have to create a single-column layout. I hope you already have an idea how to achieve it in the aforementioned code. For extra small screens, we have to use classes that have the `col-xs` prefix. Here, we want each blog post columns to occupy all the 12 Bootstrap columns so that we have only one blog post in each row. Our class will be `col-xs-12`, so let's proceed and add this class to our code:

```
<div class="container">
    <div class="row">
        <div class="col-md-12 text-center">
            <h1>My First Bootstrap Blog</h1>
        </div>
    </div>

    <hr>

    <div class="row">
        <div class="col-md-4 col-sm-6 col-xs-12">
            <h3>Post Title 1</h3>
            <p>Lorem ipsum dolor sit amet ... </p>
        </div>
        <div class="col-md-4 col-sm-6 col-xs-12">
            <h3>Post Title 2</h3>
            <p>Lorem ipsum dolor sit amet ... </p>
        </div>
        <div class="col-md-4 col-sm-6 col-xs-12">
            <h3>Post Title 3</h3>
            <p>Lorem ipsum dolor sit amet ... </p>
        </div>
        <div class="col-md-4 col-sm-6 col-xs-12">
            <h3>Post Title 4</h3>
            <p>Lorem ipsum dolor sit amet ... </p>
        </div>
        <div class="col-md-4 col-sm-6 col-xs-12">
            <h3>Post Title 5</h3>
            <p>Lorem ipsum dolor sit amet ... </p>
        </div>
        <div class="col-md-4 col-sm-6 col-xs-12">
            <h3>Post Title 6</h3>
```

```
                <p>Lorem ipsum dolor sit amet ... </p>
          </div>
      </div>
</div>
```

Figure 2.12. A 1-column layout on small screens

Finally, we have a complete HTML page that is responsive and works on any kind of display—the one-column layout is shown in Figure 2.12. You can even host this project using a free cloud-based service such as Google Drive[1] and then test it on an actual tablet or mobile device; alternatively, manually resize the browser width

---

[1] https://drive.google.com/

and watch the layout change dynamically. I hope you found this case study useful in understanding Bootstrap's grid system.

Nesting Columns

You can always create a new set of 12 Bootstrap columns within any column in your layout. This can be done by building a new row element within an existing column and then filling this row with custom columns. Since we are starting a new row here, any column within it can also span across 12 Bootstrap columns, but the width of this row will be restricted to its parent's width.

Let's illustrate this with an example. Make a new HTML file in the project called **nested.html**. Form the HTML markup with Bootstrap set up in it as discussed in the last chapter. In addition, link the CSS file **styles.css** that we created earlier in this chapter. The markup of this new HTML file should look this:

```
<!DOCTYPE html>
    <html lang="en">
      <head>
        <meta charset="utf-8">
        <meta http-equiv="X-UA-Compatible" content="IE=edge">
        <meta name="viewport" content="width=device-width,
➥initial-scale=1">

        <title>My First Bootstrap Website</title>
        <link rel="stylesheet" type="text/css"
➥href="css/bootstrap.css">

        <!--[if lt IE 9]>
          <script src="https://oss.maxcdn.com/libs/html5shiv/
➥3.7.0/html5shiv.js"></script>
          <script src="https://oss.maxcdn.com/libs/respond.js/
➥1.4.2/respond.min.js"></script>
        <![endif]-->

      </head>
      <body>

          <script src="js/jquery.js"></script>
```

```
        <script src="js/bootstrap.js"></script>
    </body>
  </html>
```

Let's create a `container` and a row within it:

```
<div class="container">
    <div class="row">

    </div>
</div>
```

Targeting medium-sized displays, we'll construct a two-column layout. By now, we know that to create a two-column layout, we should span our columns to six Bootstrap columns. Hence, the class for generating such columns will be `col-md-6`. Let's add two columns to the previous markup:

```
<div class="container">
    <div class="row">
        <div class="col-md-6 col1">
            <h3>Column 1</h3>
        </div>
        <div class="col-md-6 col2">
            <h3>Column 2</h3>
        </div>
    </div>
</div>
```

In this code, we have also pulled two classes from our **styles.css** file: `col1` and `col2`. These two classes will help us provide some background color to our columns. Now the HTML page should look like the screenshot in Figure 2.13.

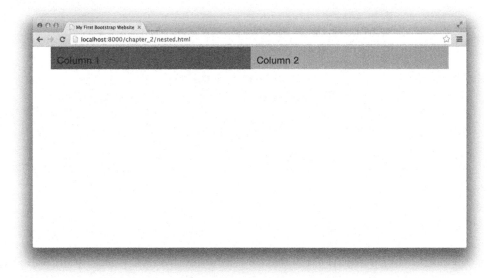

Figure 2.13. A simple two-column layout

Let's now nest the first column "Column 1" and start a new row within it:

```
<div class="container">
    <div class="row">
        <div class="col-md-6 col1">
            <h3>Column 1</h3>
            <!-- Nesting Starts -->
            <div class="row">

            </div>
        </div>
        <div class="col-md-6 col2">
            <h3>Column 2</h3>
        </div>
    </div>
</div>
```

As we have a new row, let's form two columns again within it:

```
<div class="container">
    <div class="row">
        <div class="col-md-6 col1">
            <h3>Column 1</h3>
            <!-- Nesting Starts -->
```

```
                    <div class="row">
                        <div class="col-md-6 col3">
                            <h3>Column 4</h3>
                        </div>
                        <div class="col-md-6 col4">
                            <h3>Column 5</h3>
                        </div>
                    </div>
                </div>
                <div class="col-md-6 col2">
                    <h3>Column 2</h3>
                </div>
            </div>
        </div>
    </div>
</div>
```

As you can see in Figure 2.14, the two new columns are now placed within the first column. Here I have used the classes col3 and col4 from **styles.css** to apply the background color.

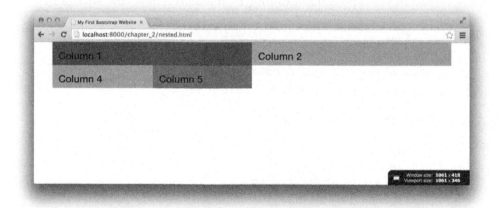

Figure 2.14. Nested two-column layout

The ability to nest columns comes in handy when creating complex layouts. You can also further nest the innermost row and generate a new set of columns within it. This process can continue until you achieve the desired layout.

Offsetting Columns

Offsetting is another great feature of Bootstrap's grid system. It is generally used to increase the left margin of a column. For example, if you have a column that should appear after a gap of three Bootstrap columns, you can use the offsetting feature.

Classes that are available for offsetting are:

- `col-xs-offset-*`
- `col-sm-offset-*`
- `col-md-offset-*`
- `col-lg-offset-*`

Suppose we want to move a column three Bootstrap columns towards the right in extra-small displays, we can use the class `"col-xs-offset-3"`, for example:

```
<div class="row">
    <div class="col-xs-6 col-xs-offset-3 col1">
        <h1>Hello Learnable!</h1>
    </div>
</div>
```

This code will result in a column that spans to six Bootstrap columns, offset three columns towards the right as shown in Figure 2.15.

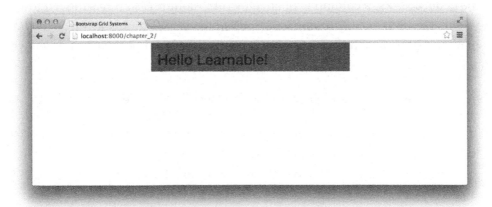

Figure 2.15. An offset column

Centering Your Column

Note that there's a three-column gap on both the left and right side of this column. This is one of the best ways of centering a 50% width column in the middle of the screen.

Reordering Grids Manually

We can also reorder the columns irrespective of the order in which they're written in the code. If we have written a `col-md-9` column first and then a `col-md-3` column, we can easily swap their position when the HTML page is rendered by a browser. This is done using Bootstrap's `pull` and `push` classes.

Classes such as `col-xs-pull-*` and `col-xs-push-*` are used to move a column towards the left and right respectively by a certain number of columns. For example:

```
<div class="row">
    <div class="col-xs-9 col-xs-push-3">
        <h1>Pushed Column</h1>
    </div>
    <div class="col-xs-3 col-xs-pull-9">
        <h1>Pulled Column</h1>
    </div>
</div>
```

In the code, `col-xs-9` column is pushed by three columns so it has moved towards the right. The `col-xs-3` column is also pulled by nine columns towards the left. Hence, they appear as if they have swapped their original position when viewed on a browser.

There are several variants of `push` and `pull` classes as per the screen size:

- `col-xs-pull-*` and `col-xs-push-*` for extra smaller screens
- `col-sm-pull-*` and `col-sm-push-*` for smaller screens
- `col-md-pull-*` and `col-md-push-*` for medium screens
- `col-lg-pull-*` and `col-lg-push-*` for larger screens

You can replace * with an integer between one and 12 depending on the number of columns you want to `pull` or `push` them.

Summary

You can produce almost any kind of website layout using Bootstrap's grid system. If used properly you can design a beautiful and responsive website that works in almost any kind of display device. Features like nesting, offsetting and reordering also make it more powerful.

For more documentation on Bootstrap's grid system, refer to http://getbootstrap.com/css/#grid.

Exploring Bootstrap Components

In this chapter, we'll start using some of Bootstrap's most useful HTML **components**. Components such as buttons, headers, navigation menus, and comments system are commonly found on websites. Through its components, Bootstrap helps us add such features to our sites quickly and easily.

Page Components

Page components form the basic structure of a web page. Examples of page components include page headers, standout panels for displaying important information, nested comments sections, image thumbnails, and stacked lists of links. These are popular components that can take quite a while to develop from scratch.

In this section, we'll focus on creating reusable HTML components using Bootstrap-recommended markup and classes. Let's start with page headers.

Page Headers

Giving a page a heading or title is not a big deal. Anyone can use an <h1> tag to display a heading on a web page; however, to neatly display a title with cleared browser default styles, the proper amount of spacing around it, and a small subtitle beside it can consume a surprising amount of time.

Fortunately, Bootstrap has created an HTML component to be used as a **page header** that takes care of all these additional tasks for us. Before we check out the markup for the page header, let's first set up the project that we'll be using throughout this chapter.

First, copy the contents of the folder **Bootstrap_demos** and paste them into a new folder called **Chapter_3**. Open the **index.html** file and remove the <h1> tag that is present inside the <body> tag.

Now, let's add the markup for a page header:

```
<div class="page-header">
    <h1>Chapter 3</h1>
</div>
```

Whenever you want to use the <h1> tag for a page title, you can wrap it in a <div> element that has a class of page-header to create a page header component.

Now let's view **index.html** in our browser. It should look like Figure 3.1.

Figure 3.1. A basic page header

As you can see, the page header component doesn't add any additional styles for the h1 other than a thin gray bottom border. It only comes with styles for adding subtitles, which we'll see soon.

A small issue that we see here is that the page header has stuck to the browser's left border. That's because we haven't defined a container for all the contents of our web page. So let's create a global container:

```
<div class="container">

</div>
```

Now place the page header markup inside the container div. Our final markup should look like this:

```
<div class="container">
    <div class="page-header">
        <h1>Chapter 3</h1>
    </div>
</div>
```

And the result can be seen in Figure 3.2.

Figure 3.2. Our header in a container

If you want to add a subtitle beside the title of the page, you can put it inside the same <h1> tag that we used before. Make sure you wrap the subtitle inside a <small></small> tag, like so:

```
<div class="container">
    <div class="page-header">
        <h1>Chapter 3 <small>Exploring Bootstrap Components
➥</small></h1>
    </div>
</div>
```

The effect can be seen in Figure 3.3.

Figure 3.3. Header with subtitle

Panels

Panels are used to display text or images within a box with rounded corners. Here's how to create a panel, and what it looks like in Figure 3.4:

```
<div class="panel panel-default">
    <div class="panel-heading">
      ATTENTION
    </div>
    <div class="panel-body">
      Lorem ipsum dolor sit ametnim ...
    </div>
    <div class="panel-footer">
      <a href="#" class="btn btn-danger btn-sm">Agree</a>
```

```
➥<a href="#" class="btn btn-default btn-sm">Decline</a>
    </div>
</div>
```

Figure 3.4. A panel

As you can see, the panel `div` has been divided into three parts: the `panel-head`, `panel-body`, and `panel-footer`. Each of these panel parts is optional.

Panels come with various color options. In the previous code, I've used the default color with the help of the `panel-default` class. You can also use other classes for different colors:

- `panel-primary` for dark blue
- `panel-success` for green
- `panel-info` for sky blue
- `panel-warning` for yellow
- `panel-danger` for red

Media Object

Media object is used for creating components that should contain left- or right-aligned media (image, video, or audio) alongside some textual content. It is best suited for creating features such as a comments section, displaying tweets, or showing product details where a product image is present.

Designing a comments section for your website can be a tricky task. You need to carefully design some reusable HTML markup that supports nested commenting. Bootstrap's media object comes in handy here, as you can quite easily create multiple levels of nested comments using it.

The markup for creating a media object is:

```
<div class="media">
    <a class="pull-left" href="#">
        <img class="media-object" src="path/to/image"
➥alt="Syed Fazle Rahman">
    </a>
    <div class="media-body">
        <h4 class="media-heading">Awesome piece of work!</h4>
        <p>Lorem ipsum dolor sit amet, consectetur ...</p>
    </div>
</div>
```

To produce a media object you need to create a div with a class of `media`. Then you put two necessary components within it: the **media** itself (here it's an image) and the `media-body`. As seen from the code snippet, the media should have the class `media-object` and be wrapped within an `<a></a>` tag. You can then align the media to either side by adding a `pull-left` or `pull-right` class to the a element.

Next, the `media-body` div should have two further components: the title and the textual content. The title can be given using an h4 element with a `media-heading` class and the textual content is represented using a p element.

That's it! Go ahead and view it in the browser; it should look like Figure 3.5.

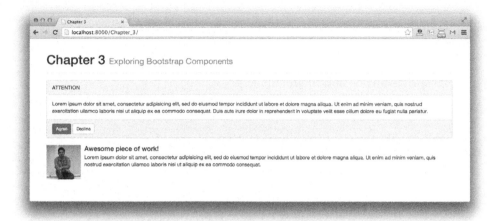

Figure 3.5. A media object

To create a nested comments design, we can place more media object markup inside the media-body div of the previous media object as follows:

```
<div class="media">
    <a class="pull-left" href="#">
        <img class="media-object" src="path/to/image"
➥alt="Syed Fazle Rahman">
    </a>
    <div class="media-body">
        <h4 class="media-heading">Awesome piece of work!</h4>
        <p>Lorem ipsum dolor sit amet, consectetur ...</p>

        <!-- Second Media Object -->
        <div class="media">
            <a class="pull-left" href="#">
                <img class="media-object" src="path/to/image"
➥alt="Syed Fazle Rahman">
            </a>
            <div class="media-body">
                <h4 class="media-heading">Awesome piece of
➥work!</h4>
                <p>Lorem ipsum dolor sit amet, consectetur ...</p>
            </div>
        </div>
```

```
      </div>
  </div>
```

Figure 3.6 shows our nested media object.

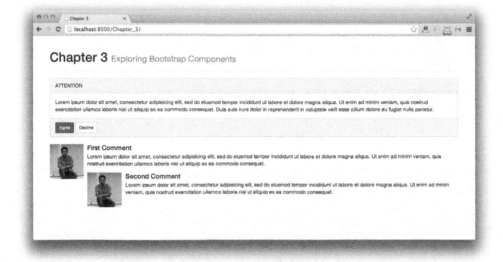

Figure 3.6. Nested media object

You can use as many nesting levels as you wish.

Thumbnails

Displaying images and video thumbnails is a snap with Bootstrap's **thumbnails** component. It is used for displaying images and videos with clickable appeal by applying a border that forms a box around them. It also comes with a neat hover effect that highlights the focused thumbnail by changing its border color to blue.

Here's the markup for creating a thumbnail:

```
<a href="#" class="thumbnail">
    <img src="path/to/image">
</a>
```

Let's create a four-column design using Bootstrap's grid system. We'll place an image in each column and then apply thumbnail markup to each one.

As seen in the previous chapter, we'll use the class `col-xs-3` to create a four- column design:

```
<div class="row">
    <div class="col-xs-3">
        <a href="#" class="thumbnail">
            <img src="path/to/image">
        </a>
    </div>
    <div class="col-xs-3">
        <a href="#" class="thumbnail">
            <img src="path/to/image">
        </a>
    </div>
    <div class="col-xs-3">
        <a href="#" class="thumbnail">
            <img src="path/to/image">
        </a>
    </div>
    <div class="col-xs-3">
        <a href="#" class="thumbnail">
            <img src="path/to/image">
        </a>
    </div>
</div>
```

This produces the result shown in Figure 3.7.

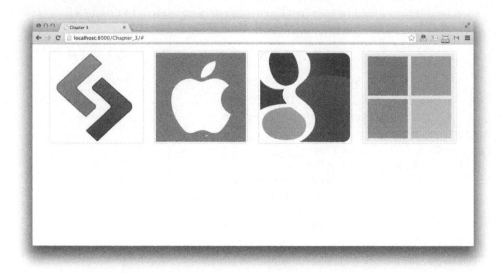

Figure 3.7. Thumbnails

Try hovering your mouse icon over each image and you should get a nice highlighted effect. In the aforementioned code, you can see that I have applied the class thumbnail to an anchor tag <a>. You can also use a <div> tag instead of an anchor to represent a thumbnail.

Let's give a caption to each thumbnail. We just need to add an extra div with class caption just below the <img> tag. Our snippet for a thumbnail with a caption should be:

```
<a href="#" class="thumbnail">
    <img src="path/to/image">
    <div class="caption">
        <h3>Caption Goes Here!</h3>
    </div>
</a>
```

If you apply a caption to each thumbnail on the page, it will produce a similar result to Figure 3.8.

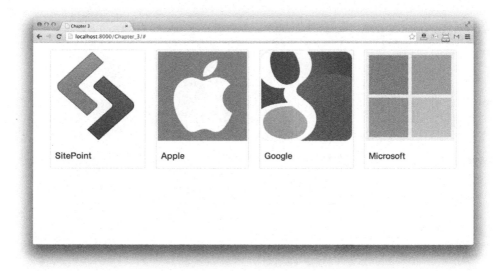

Figure 3.8. Thumbnails with captions

You can also add some excerpts to each thumbnail and a **Read More** button for linking to different pages in your website. For this we need to first replace the link element with the class `thumbnail` with a `div` element. Then we add an excerpt using `<p>` inside the "`caption`" div and a link with a "`Read More`" anchor and classes `btn` and `btn-primary` inside the same "`caption`" div. After making these changes, our final markup for a post thumbnail will be as follows:

```
<div class="thumbnail">
    <img src="images/microsoft.png">
    <div class="caption">
        <h3>Microsoft</h3>
        <p>Lorem ipsum dolor sit amet, consectetur ...</p>
        <p><a href="#" class="btn btn-primary">Read More</a></p>
    </div>
</div>
```

The above code will produce a result similar to Figure 3.9.

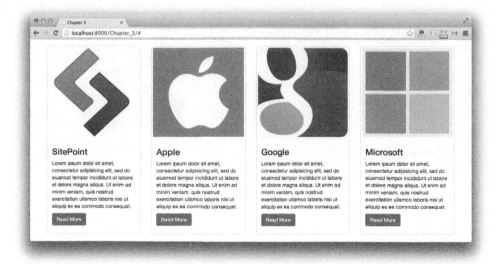

Figure 3.9. Captions with "Read More" links

List Group

List group is a useful component for creating lists, such as a list of useful resources or a list of recent activities. You can also use it for a complex list of large amounts of textual content.

The markup for creating a list group is as follows, with the result shown directly below in Figure 3.10:

```
<ul class="list-group">
    <li class="list-group-item">Inbox</li>
    <li class="list-group-item">Sent</li>
    <li class="list-group-item">Drafts</li>
```

```
    <li class="list-group-item">Deleted</li>
    <li class="list-group-item">Spam</li>
</ul>
```

Figure 3.10. A list group

You need to add the class `list-group` to a `ul` element or a `div` element to make its children appear as a list. The children can be `li` elements or `a` elements, depending on your parent element choice. The child should always have the class `list-group-item`.

Lists of Links

When you want to display a list of links, you should use the anchor element `a` instead of list elements `li` (that also means using a parent `div`, instead of a `ul`).

We can also display a number (such as those used to indicate pending notifications) beside each list item using the badge component. We'll learn more about badges later in this chapter, but for now you can add the following snippet inside each "`list-group-item`" to display a number beside each one:

```
<span class="badge">14</span>
```

So our updated list group will now look like Figure 3.11.

Figure 3.11. Updated list group

As you can see, the badges beautifully align themselves to the right of each list item.

We can also apply various colors to each list item by adding `list-group-item-*` classes along with `list-group-item`. They are as follows:

- `list-group-item-success` for green
- `list-group-item-info` for sky blue
- `list-group-item-warning` for pale yellow
- `list-group-item-danger` for light red

For example, adding `list-group-item-success` to the `list-group-item` class in the following list will give it a light green background color:

```
<li class="list-group-item list-group-item-success">Inbox</li>
```

We can do more with list groups than just construct straightforward lists, though. If you want to create a list in which each list item contains some textual content along with a heading, you could use the following markup:

```
<a href="#" class="list-group-item">
    <h4 class="list-group-item-heading">Item heading</h4>
    <p class="list-group-item-text">Lorem ipsum dolor sit ...</p>
</a>
```

Instead of just text, we are now placing a set of h4 and p elements in each `list-group-item` element. We're using the classes `list-group-item-heading` and `list-group-item-text` for h4 and p elements respectively to display them appropriately, seen in Figure 3.12.

Figure 3.12. A list group with text

You can also highlight any element in the list using an additional class `active`. Here, I have highlighted the first element.

Navigation Components

Features such as navigation bars and breadcrumbs have become an essential part of many websites. Bootstrap comes with many components built in to help build such features. Let's proceed and create our first navigation component.

Navs

Navs are a group of links that are placed inline with each other to be used for navigation. We have options to make this group of links appear either as tabs or small buttons, the latter known as **pills** in Bootstrap. We will first learn how to create tab-like links and then proceed to create pill-like links.

We create tab-like navigation links like so:

```
<ul class="nav nav-tabs">
    <li class="active"><a href="#">About</a></li>
    <li><a href="#">Activity</a></li>
    <li><a href="#">Liked Pages</a></li>
</ul>
```

Here's a screenshot of what they look like(Figure 3.13).

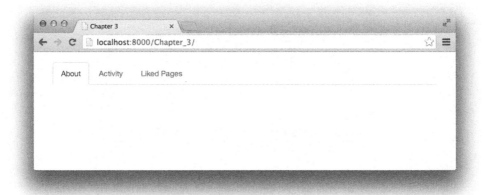

Figure 3.13. Tab-like navigation

The class `nav` is common to both tabs and pills. We've added the `nav-tabs` class to make our navigation bar look like tabs.

We create pill-like navigation links this way (and seen following in Figure 3.14):

```
<ul class="nav nav-pills">
    <li class="active"><a href="#">About</a></li>
    <li><a href="#">Activity</a></li>
    <li><a href="#">Liked Pages</a></li>
</ul>
```

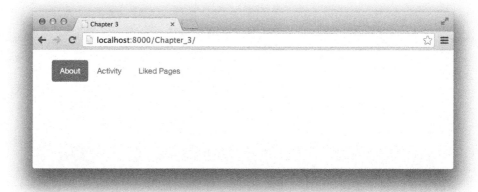

Figure 3.14. Pill-like navigation

Here, we have replaced the class nav-tabs with class nav-pills, which make the same list look like pills.

We can also vertically stack these pills by attaching an additional class nav-stacked to it:

```
<ul class="nav nav-pills nav-stacked">
    <li class="active"><a href="#">About</a></li>
    <li><a href="#">Activity</a></li>
    <li><a href="#">Liked Pages</a></li>
</ul>
```

Figure 3.15 shows some vertically stacked pill navigation.

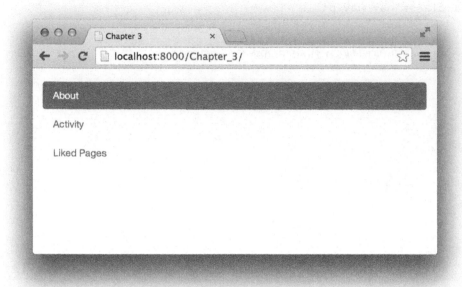

Figure 3.15. Stacked pill-like nav

Navbar

The **Navbar** is one of the most interesting Bootstrap components. Novice developers often find constructing navigation bars as one of the most daunting aspects of website development. It brings many challenges, such as ensuring proper alignment with the header as well as the rest of the body. Properly aligning links, the search bar, and drop-down menus inside a navigation bar can make the job even harder.

Bootstrap makes creating navigation bars very easy. It comes with various options to build all types of navigation bars that are responsive, automatically collapsing when the screen's size is small.

We'll first cover how to create a simple navbar with Bootstrap, and then move on to form more complex ones.

First, we'll build a `div` element, with two classes `navbar` and `navbar-default`. These classes are important to Bootstrap as they identify where to apply the navigation bar styles and effects:

```
<div class="navbar navbar-default">
</div>
```

Next, we'll use a div with class `container-fluid` inside this `navbar` element. This will wrap all the contents of the navbar and create a full-width container inside it:

```
<div class="navbar navbar-default">
    <div class="container-fluid">

    </div>
</div>
```

Now, let's start inserting other elements inside the navbar. First, we'll place a div with class `navbar-header`. This will be used for website branding purposes, such as displaying the name of the website or its logo. We'll also place a hidden button inside the `navbar-header` element that will be visible only in smaller screens where the navbar collapses. This hidden button will be later used to expand the collapsed menu in smaller screens:

```
<div class="navbar navbar-default">
    <div class="container-fluid">
        <div class="navbar-header">
            <button type="button" class="navbar-toggle"
➥data-toggle="collapse" data-target="#mynavbar-content">
                <span class="icon-bar"></span>
                <span class="icon-bar"></span>
                <span class="icon-bar"></span>
            </button>
            <a class="navbar-brand" href="#">SitePoint</a>
        </div>
    </div>
</div>
```

In the code, we have placed a button with a class `navbar-toggle` that is used by Bootstrap to activate the navbar's toggling behavior. It should have two custom data-* type attributes: `data-toggle` and `data-target`. `data-toggle` tells the script what to do when the button is clicked, whereas `data-target` tells which section to toggle when clicked. Here, the `data-target` attribute is holding an id of a section that we're yet to define. That section will be toggled when the button is clicked. The `span` elements inside the button are used for displaying the icon.

We have also defined an a element with class `navbar-brand` that holds the name of our website. At this point, you should check what the code renders to in your browser. It should display as shown in Figure 3.16.

Figure 3.16. A navbar

Try resizing the browser window to a smaller size. You should see the navbar displaying the hidden button on smaller windows, as shown in Figure 3.17.

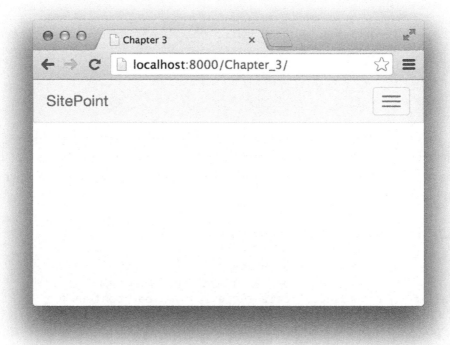

Figure 3.17. Our navbar on smaller displays

Next, we'll create another div that will be the sibling of navbar-header; that is, it is present at the same level in the markup hierarchy. We will give two classes to this element: collapse and navbar-collapse. As this div will contain all the navbar content, we'll give the id mynavbar-content to it, the same id that is mentioned inside the data-toggle attribute of the hidden button. The code should now look like this:

```
<div class="navbar navbar-default">
    <div class="container-fluid">
        <div class="navbar-header">
            <button type="button" class="navbar-toggle"
➥data-toggle="collapse" data-target="#mynavbar-content">
            <span class="icon-bar"></span>
            <span class="icon-bar"></span>
            <span class="icon-bar"></span>
        </button>
        <a class="navbar-brand" href="#">Sitepoint</a>
```

```
        </div>

        <div class="collapse navbar-collapse" id="mynavbar-content">

        </div>
    </div>
</div>
```

Now let's start filling up the navbar-collapse element with the set of links we want to place inside the navigation bar. We'll use the ul element with classes nav and navbar-nav here. These classes are used to align the links properly with the navigation bar:

```
<div class="navbar navbar-default">
    <div class="container-fluid">
        <div class="navbar-header">
          <button type="button" class="navbar-toggle"
➥data-toggle="collapse" data-target="#mynavbar-content">
            <span class="icon-bar"></span>
            <span class="icon-bar"></span>
            <span class="icon-bar"></span>
          </button>
          <a class="navbar-brand" href="#">SitePoint</a>
        </div>

        <div class="collapse navbar-collapse" id="mynavbar-content">
            <ul class="nav navbar-nav">
                <li class="active"><a href="#">Home</a></li>
                <li><a href="#">About</a></li>
                <li><a href="#">Pricing</a></li>
                <li><a href="#">Contact</a></li>
                <li><a href="#">Feedback</a></li>
            </ul>
        </div>
    </div>
</div>
```

Our final navbar with links should look like Figure 3.18.

Figure 3.18. Final navbar

You can also try resizing the browser and use the hidden button to show the menu in a smaller screen. You should have something similar to Figure 3.19.

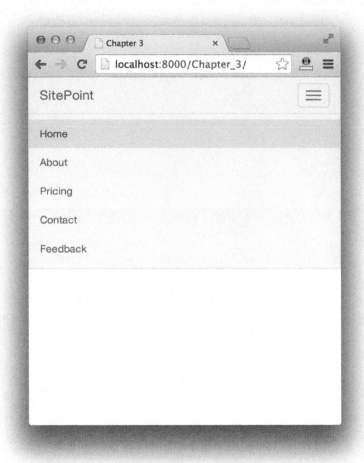

Figure 3.19. Resized navbar

Amazing, no? You have created a highly responsive navigation bar without writing a single line of CSS or JavaScript code.

Later in this chapter, we'll see how to design a form in Bootstrap. You can directly place that form within the `navbar-collapse` element to show it inside the navigation bar.

Drop-down menus are another important component of any navigation bar we see today. You can easily convert one of the `li` elements of the `navbar-nav` list to a drop-down menu as follows:

```
<li class="dropdown">
    <a href="#" class="dropdown-toggle" data-toggle="dropdown">
➥About <b class="caret"></b></a>
    <ul class="dropdown-menu">
        <li><a href="#">Board of Members</a></li>
        <li><a href="#">Developers Team</a></li>
        <li><a href="#">Designing Team</a></li>
        <li class="divider"></li>
        <li><a href="#">Investors</a></li>
        <li><a href="#">Share holders</a></li>
    </ul>
</li>
```

Add a class dropdown to the li that you want to make a drop-down. Then insert an additional ul list with class dropdown-menu to represent child links. Figure 3.20 shows the outcome.

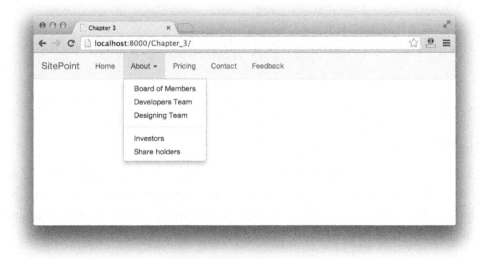

Figure 3.20. A drop-down menu

Breadcrumb

Breadcrumbs are used to show the current page's location in the site hierarchy. Bootstrap's breadcrumb component has a very simple markup and can be placed anywhere in your website:

```
<ol class="breadcrumb">
  <li><a href="#">Home</a></li>
  <li><a href="#">About</a></li>
  <li class="active">Author</li>
</ol>
```

This should result in Figure 3.21.

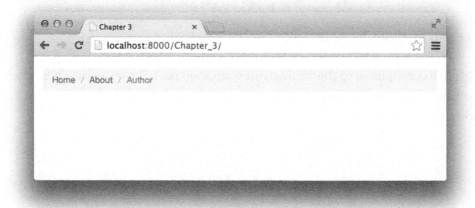

Figure 3.21. Breadcrumb

Standing Out

Sometimes we need to design components that when used with other HTML elements grab visitors' attention immediately. They can be labels, notification icons, or huge buttons such as "Buy now", "Grab it", and so on. Bootstrap ships with many such components out of the box. Let's check out some of the important ones.

Label

Labels are the best way to display short text beside other components. Sometimes we may need to display text such as "New" or "Download now", for example, beside some other HTML elements. Labels come in handy in such places.

To display a label, you need to add a `label` class to inline HTML elements such as `span` and `i`. Here, we'll use a `span` to show a label beside an `h3` element:

```
<h3>Jump Start Bootstrap <span class="label label-default">New
➡</span></h3>
```

Figure 3.22 shows what this looks like.

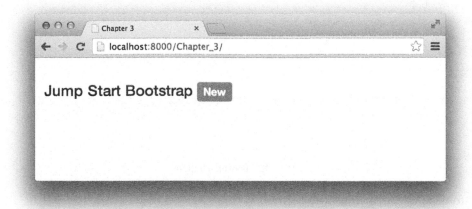

Figure 3.22. Labels

There's an additional class, `label-default`, that is necessary to tell Bootstrap which variant of label we want to use. The available label variants are:

- `label-default` for gray
- `label-primary` for dark blue
- `label-success` for green
- `label-info` for light blue
- `label-warning` for orange
- `label-danger` for red

Buttons

You can easily create a button in Bootstrap. You just have to add the `btn` class to convert an `a`, `button`, or `input` element into a fancy bold button in Bootstrap:

```
<a href="#" class="btn btn-primary">Click Here</a>
```

Figure 3.23 shows what it will look like.

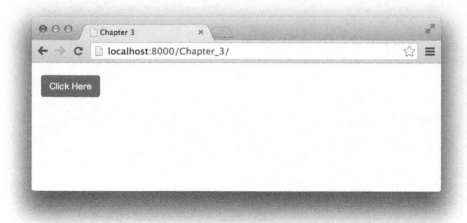

Figure 3.23. Bootstrap buttons

Buttons come in various color options:

- `btn-default` for white
- `btn-primary` for dark blue
- `btn-success` for green
- `btn-info` for light blue
- `btn-warning` for orange
- `btn-danger` for red

And in various sizes:

- `btn-lg` for large buttons
- `btn-sm` for small buttons
- `btn-xs` for extra small buttons

Here are some examples of how they can be used:

```
<button type="button" class="btn btn-primary btn-lg">Large button
➥</button>

<button type="button" class="btn btn-primary">Default button
➥</button>

<button type="button" class="btn btn-primary btn-sm">Small
```

```
➥button</button>

<button type="button" class="btn btn-primary btn-xs">Extra
➥small button</button>
```

There are some more helper classes for buttons available:

- `btn-block` will make the button span across the whole grid

- `active` will make the button look like it's currently clicked

- `disabled` will make the button unable to be clicked and appear faded. You should also be careful while using this class, as it will prevent click action on `input` and `button` elements but won't disable the click action on a elements.

Glyphicons

Glyphicons are used to display small icons. They are lightweight font icons and not images. There are many advantages of using a glyphicon instead of small images, including:

- saving multiple requests for small images or sprites

- as they are font icons, their colors and sizes can be varied on the go using CSS properties

- that they look crisp and sharp in all kind of displays.

To use glyphicons, you need to use markup like this:

```
<span class="glyphicon glyphicon-heart"></span>
```

This code displays a heart icon. Every icon in the glyphicons set comes with a unique class. You need to replace "`glyphicon-heart`" with the name of the class of the icon you want to display. A list of glyphicon icons and their classes can be found at the Bootstrap website.[1]

Glyphicon icons are designed by a freelance developer named Jan Kovařík and not by the Bootstrap developers. Most of the icons aren't free, though Kovařík has

---

[1] http://getbootstrap.com/components/#glyphicons

donated a set of icons to the Bootstrap team. You can find more font icons on his website, glyphicons.com.[2]

Wells

Wells are a useful component that wrap the content within a rounded cornered box with a gray background, giving an inset effect to the content. They can be used to highlight important facts amongst long textual content, for example, or an author's bio box in a blogging application:

```
<div class="well">
    <p>Lorem ipsum dolor sit amet, consectetur ... </p>
</div>
```

Here's the effect in Figure 3.24.

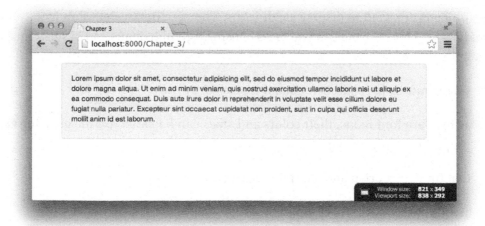

Figure 3.24. Wells

You may be unsatisfied with the amount of spacing around the content. Fortunately, Bootstrap has a solution for that too! Wells comes in three variants:

1. Default: use only the well class.
2. Large spacing: use the well and well-lg classes together.
3. Small spacing: use the well and well-sm classes together.

---

[2] http://glyphicons.com

Badges

Badges are similar to the labels that we have already discussed, but there's a major difference: labels are rectangular in shape, whereas badges are more rounded. Badges are mostly used to display numbers such as unread items, notifications, and so on, rather than text.

Badges are **self-collapsing** components, which means when there's no content inside the badge it will not be visible on the website.

The markup for a badge component looks like this:

```
<span class="badge">23</span>
```

A more custom usage of a badge is:

```
<a href="#" class="btn btn-primary btn-lg">Inbox
➥<span class="badge">23</span></a>
```

And you can see the output in Figure 3.25.

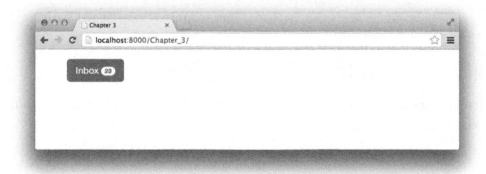

Figure 3.25. Badges

That ends our discussion on the stand out components of Bootstrap. Though these components are not essential to create great responsive websites, they definitely provide additional value for your visitors. Let's now check out how creating forms has become even easier in Bootstrap.

Fun with Forms

Forms are a very important part of our websites. They are used in the registration and login pages, contact and feedback pages, search boxes, and many other places.

Bootstrap allows you to create various types of forms within minutes. You can also use many of HTML5's form validation attributes that are well supported by Bootstrap. So let's build our first basic form.

Basic Form

To construct a form, we need a `form` element with the `form` class added to it:

```
<form class="form">
</form>
```

For each label and input field, we require a `form-group` classed `div` element. Let's create an input field that will ask our visitors their name:

```
<form class="form">
    <div class="form-group">
        <label for="nameField">Name</label>
        <input type="text" class="form-control" id="nameField"
➥placeholder="Your Name" />
    </div>
</form>
```

Attaching the class `form-control` to an `input` element will make it a full-width element, seen in Figure 3.26.

Figure 3.26. A basic form

Let's fill the form with email, phone number, and textarea fields and, finally, a submit button. The complete markup and screenshot in Figure 3.27 follows:

```
<form class="form">
    <div class="form-group">
        <label for="nameField">Name</label>
        <input type="text" class="form-control" id="nameField"
➡placeholder="Your Name" />
    </div>

    <div class="form-group">
        <label for="emailField">Email</label>
        <input type="email" class="form-control" id="emailField"
➡placeholder="Your Email" />
    </div>

    <div class="form-group">
        <label for="phoneField">Phone</label>
        <input type="text" class="form-control" id="phoneField"
➡placeholder="Your Phone Number" />
    </div>

    <div class="form-group">
        <label for="descField">Description</label>
        <textarea class="form-control" id="descField" placeholder="
➡Your Comments"></textarea>
    </div>
```

```
    <button type="submit" class="btn btn-primary">Submit</button>
➥<button type="reset" class="btn btn-default">Reset</button>
</form>
```

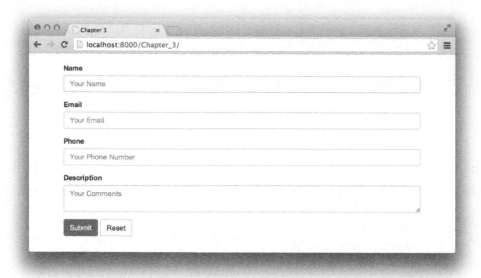

Figure 3.27. Form with added fields

Horizontal Forms

In the previous form, we have displayed a label on top and then the input field.
Suppose we want to display the labels to the side of the input fields instead. Then
we can use Bootstrap's grid system inside the form element, like so:

```
<form class="form-horizontal">
    <div class="form-group">
        <label for="nameField" class="col-xs-2">Name</label>
        <div class="col-xs-10">
            <input type="text" class="form-control" id="nameField"
➥placeholder="Your Name" />
        </div>
    </div>

    <div class="form-group">
        <label for="emailField" class="col-xs-2">Email</label>
        <div class="col-xs-10">
            <input type="email" class="form-control" id="emailField"
```

```
➥placeholder="Your Email" />
        </div>
    </div>

    <div class="form-group">
        <label for="phoneField" class="col-xs-2">Phone</label>
        <div class="col-xs-10">
            <input type="text" class="form-control" id="phoneField"
➥placeholder="Your Phone Number" />
        </div>
    </div>

    <div class="form-group">
        <label for="descField" class="col-xs-2">Description</label>
        <div class="col-xs-10">
            <textarea class="form-control" id="descField"
➥placeholder="Your Comments"></textarea>
        </div>
    </div>

    <div class="col-xs-10 col-xs-offset-2">
        <button type="submit" class="btn btn-primary">Submit
➥</button> <button type="reset" class="btn btn-default">Reset
➥</button>
    </div>

</form>
```

This should produce the horizontal form shown in Figure 3.28.

Figure 3.28. A horizontal form

In the code, we have replaced the form's class from `form` to `form-horizontal` as per Bootstrap's rules. Then we have added a class `col-xs-2` to the `label` element so that it spans across two Bootstrap columns. Next, we have wrapped the input field inside a div that spans across ten Bootstrap columns with the help of class `col-xs-10`.

Inline Form

We can also create forms whose elements are present in a single line. An example is a login form in the top navigation bar where both the username and password fields are placed side-by-side.

The markup for an inline form is as follows:

```
<div class="well well-sm">
    <form class="form-inline">
        <div class="form-group">
            <input type="email" class="form-control" id="emailField"
➥placeholder="Enter email">
        </div>

        <div class="form-group">
            <input type="password" class="form-control"
➥id="passwordField" placeholder="Password">
        </div>
```

```
        <div class="checkbox">
            <label>
                <input type="checkbox"> Remember me
            </label>
        </div>

        <button type="submit" class="btn btn-primary">Sign in
➥</button>
        </form>
</div>
```

This should produce the inline form shown in Figure 3.29.

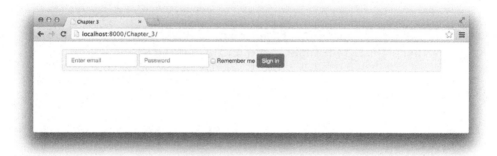

Figure 3.29. Inline form

The only major difference between an inline form and the previous forms is the name of the class. We have replaced the class `form` with `form-inline` to make the form elements inline. In the previous code, we have also wrapped the whole form content within a well component to make it look even better.

If you look carefully in the above code, you'll see that I have not used `form-group` for displaying a checkbox element. For proper alignment of a checkbox and the text beside it, you should wrap both of them inside a div classed as `checkbox`. In such cases, you should also place the `input` elements inside the `label` elements so that the click-on text is properly mapped to the corresponding `input` element.

In case you need a radio button instead of a checkbox, replace the class `checkbox` with `radio`:

```
<div class="radio">
  <label>
    <input type="radio" value="Male">
    Male
  </label>
</div>
```

Helper Classes in Forms

There are several additional "helper"classes available from Bootstrap that help in displaying forms properly.

If you have used the `disabled` attribute to disable an input element, Bootstrap has a style defined for it. For example, this code:

```
<input class="form-control" type="text"
➥placeholder="Disabled input here..." disabled>
```

will look like Figure 3.30.

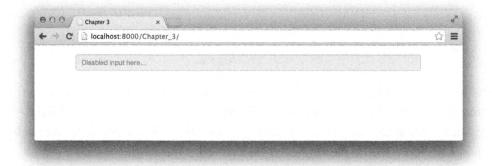

Figure 3.30. Disabled form inputs

Bootstrap also has three validation states for input elements:

1. `has-success`
2. `has-error`
3. `has-warning`

Here's an example of how validation state can be used:

```
<div class="form-group has-success">
    <label class="control-label" for="inputField">
➥Input with success</label>
    <input type="text" class="form-control" id="inputField">
</div>
```

Applying has-success will make the label text and border field green in color. Similarly, has-warning will employ a dull brown color and has-danger will use dark red. These has-* type classes will only apply colors to form-control, control-label, and help-block classed elements. If you want to show some custom text when a user enters invalid values in the input field, use a span element with class help-block. The help-block will appear below its corresponding input field when invalid values are entered.

Control Sizing

You can vary the height of input elements using the **control sizing** classes of Bootstrap:

- input-lg for bigger input elements than the default size.

- input-sm for smaller input elements than the default size.

Here's some examples of them in use:

```
<input class="form-control input-lg" type="text"
➥placeholder="Larger Input Field">
<input class="form-control" type="text"
➥placeholder="Default Input Field">
<input class="form-control input-sm" type="text"
➥placeholder="Smaller Input Field">
```

that should result in the output shown in Figure 3.31.

Figure 3.31. Control sizing

Summary

In this chapter, we have seen a collection of reusable Bootstrap components that are ready to use. As you've seen, there are a large number of different components available in Bootstrap, and initially, you may find it difficult to remember so many different types of classes; however, you can always refer to the documentation for reference whenever you land in trouble.[3]

---

[3] http://getbootstrap.com/components

Chapter

4

Bootstrap Plugins for Fun and Profit

JavaScript is the *de facto* scripting language of the Web. Beautiful image slideshows, drop-down menus, and popovers are just some examples of popular website features that can be created by combining JavaScript with CSS. In this chapter, we'll check out some of the ready-to-use JavaScript plugins that Bootstrap 3 provides for us, making it easy to create such advanced website features.

There are two different ways of using Bootstrap's JavaScript plugins. The first method requires no JavaScript at all. You just have to follow some recommended HTML markup to use them. The other method needs some JavaScript knowledge for initializing and customizing the plugins. We'll discuss both methods of using plugins, and you can decide which one suits you best.

All the plugins that we're going to use in this chapter are included in the `boot-strap.js` or `bootstrap.min.js`. If you have followed the instructions for download-ing Bootstrap in Chapter 1, you should find **bootstrap.js** inside the **/js** folder of the project.

Before proceeding, let's set up a new project for this chapter. We'll be using the same folder that we created in Chapter 1, **Bootstrap_demos**. Copy all the files in this folder and paste them inside a new folder named **Chapter 4**. Open **index.html** using text editor. Change the text inside the `<title>` tag to read "Bootstrap Plugins". Next, remove the `<h1>` tag from the body. Finally, the **index.html** file should look like this:

```
<!DOCTYPE html>
<html lang="en">
  <head>
    <meta charset="utf-8">
    <meta http-equiv="X-UA-Compatible" content="IE=edge">
    <meta name="viewport" content="width=device-width,
➥initial-scale=1">

    <title>Bootstrap Plugins</title>
    <link rel="stylesheet" type="text/css" href="css/bootstrap.css">

    <!--[if lt IE 9]>
      <script src="https://oss.maxcdn.com/libs/html5shiv/
➥3.7.0/html5shiv.js"></script>
      <script src="https://oss.maxcdn.com/libs/respond.js/
➥1.4.2/respond.min.js"></script>
    <![endif]-->

  </head>
  <body>


    <script src="js/jquery.js"></script>
    <script src="js/bootstrap.js"></script>
  </body>
</html>
```

Extending Functionality

Imagine a menu bar without any drop-down functionality. Kind of boring, right? Gone are the days when a navigation bar used to consist of just a simple list of links. In this section, we are going to use some of Bootstrap's JavaScript plugins that will help in extending the functionality of the existing components of our website. We will see how to add drop-down menus to navigation bars, the ability to toggle the states of buttons when clicked, beautiful alert messages that vanish after being displayed for some time, and more.

Dropdowns

The markup for creating a **dropdown** is as follows:

```
<div class="dropdown">
    <a data-toggle="dropdown" data-target="#"
➥href="http://www.google.com">
        Dropdown <span class="caret"></span>
    </a>
    <ul class="dropdown-menu">
        <li><a href="#">Link 1</a></li>
        <li><a href="#">Link 2</a></li>
        <li><a href="#">Link 3</a></li>
        <li><a href="#">Link 4</a></li>
    </ul>
</div>
```

Every dropdown should have two important elements: an `a` element and a `ul` element. Here the `ul` element is hidden by default and the `a` element is used to toggle the dropdown menu. The `a` element has two necessary `data-*` attributes: `data-toggle` and `data-target`. The `data-toggle` attribute tells Bootstrap to activate the dropdown effect on the link element whenever clicked. On the other hand, the `data-target` attribute is used to prevent the page redirection when a link is clicked. It's unnecessary to provide an `href` attribute here, as it will be ignored. This link element should contain some anchor text, such as "Dropdown" , and a down arrow icon, which is produced using a class of `caret`.

 Is the Caret a Glyphicon?

The caret class is not a glyphicon class. Bootstrap has written special CSS styles for the class `caret` that will produce this down arrow icon. If you want to learn how they did it, open the `bootstrap.css` file and search for "`.caret`" You will find a set of CSS properties associated with it.

You can also use a glyphicon instead of this down arrow. For that you need to replace the markup of the caret with the markup of a glyphicon:

```
<span class=" glyphicon glyphicon-chevron-down"></span>
```

Once the link and icons are placed properly, you can then create a `ul` list for representing the list of links in the dropdown menu. This `ul` element should have the class `dropdown-menu`. Now, we have a simple dropdown that displays a menu when the link is clicked. We can view it in the browser as shown in Figure 4.1.

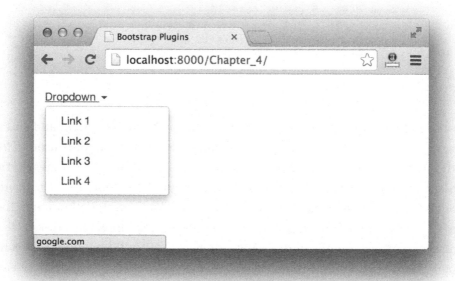

Figure 4.1. A simple dropdown menu

Let's use the dropdown plugin with the tabs and pills menus that we created in the previous chapter.

Here's the markup for the pills menu:

```
<ul class="nav nav-pills">
  <li class="active"><a href="#">Home</a></li>
  <li><a href="#">Profile</a></li>
  <li><a href="#">Messages</a></li>
</ul>
```

Let's create a dropdown plugin in the second item of the previous list:

```
<ul class="nav nav-pills">
  <li class="active"><a href="#">Home</a></li>
  <li class="dropdown">
      <a data-toggle="dropdown" data-target="#"
➥href="http://www.google.com">
          Profile <span class="caret"></span>
      </a>
      <ul class="dropdown-menu">
          <li><a href="#">Link 1</a></li>
          <li><a href="#">Link 2</a></li>
          <li><a href="#">Link 3</a></li>
          <li><a href="#">Link 4</a></li>
      </ul>
  </li>
  <li><a href="#">Messages</a></li>
</ul>
```

We have placed the whole markup of the dropdown plugin inside the second `li` element and assigned it a class `dropdown`. Hence, the above pills menu with a dropdown plugin should look like Figure 4.2.

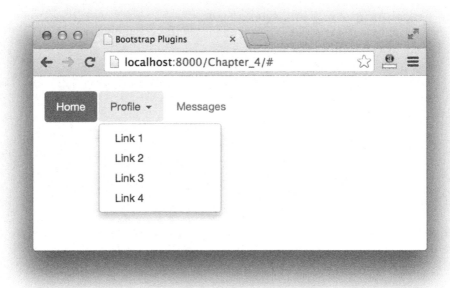

Figure 4.2. A pills menu with dropdown

You can use this dropdown plugin with any component by injecting it as shown in the previous code.

Dropdowns with JavaScript

The dropdown plugin from Bootstrap can also be used using JavaScript. Instead of providing the custom attributes such as `data-*`, you can use JavaScript objects to pass such information. Bootstrap uses the jQuery library for all JavaScript-related operations. Hence, importing `jquery.js` is crucial for using JavaScript-related customization in Bootstrap.

To trigger the dropdown plugin through jQuery, you need to use the method `dropdown()`:

```
$().dropdown('toggle');
```

We can use this method to toggle the state of the dropdown from closed to opened whenever the page loads. For example, if our code snippet for creating a dropdown is as follows:

```
<div class="dropdown" id="myDropdown">
    <a class="myDropdownHandle" data-toggle="dropdown"
➥data-target="#" href="#">
        Dropdown <span class="caret"></span>
    </a>
    <ul class="dropdown-menu">
        <li><a href="#">Link 1</a></li>
        <li><a href="#">Link 2</a></li>
        <li><a href="#">Link 3</a></li>
        <li><a href="#">Link 4</a></li>
    </ul>
</div>
```

You need to call the `dropdown()` method on the `ready()` method of jQuery:

```
<script type="text/javascript">
    $(document).ready(function(){
        $('.myDropdownHandle').dropdown('toggle');
    });
</script>
```

You can see I have used the `dropdown()` method after selecting `.myDropdownHandle`. By default, the state of a dropdown is closed; whenever you refresh the page it will toggle the state and make the menu visible.

Bootstrap provides various events attached to the dropdown plugin. They are:

- `show.bs.dropdown`: this event is triggered when the handle is just clicked; the dropdown handle has received the request to open the hidden menu

- `shown.bs.dropdown`: this event is triggered after the menu is shown

- `hide.bs.dropdown`: this event is triggered just before closing the menu

- `hidden.bs.dropdown`: this event is triggered when the menu is closed

The `show` and `hide` events happen just before completing the request whereas `shown` and `hidden` events happen as the request is complete. Here, the request was to open and close the dropdown menu.

Let me show you a demo explaining how to use these events. I have written the following jQuery snippet to target all the states of a dropdown plugin that prints a statement as each event is triggered:

```
$('#myDropdown').on('show.bs.dropdown', function () {
    console.log("Opening dropdown..");
});

$('#myDropdown').on('shown.bs.dropdown', function () {
    console.log("Dropdown opened..");
});

$('#myDropdown').on('hide.bs.dropdown', function () {
    console.log("Hiding dropdown..");
});
```

```
$('#myDropdown').on('hidden.bs.dropdown', function () {
    console.log("Dropdown hidden..");
});
```

On clicking the link handle, the console is populated with the first two messages: "Opening dropdown" and "Dropdown opened", as seen in Figure 4.3.

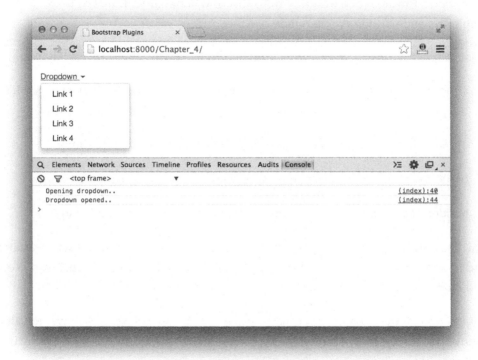

Figure 4.3. The initial click

Clicking the handle again will display the last two messages, as shown in Figure 4.4.

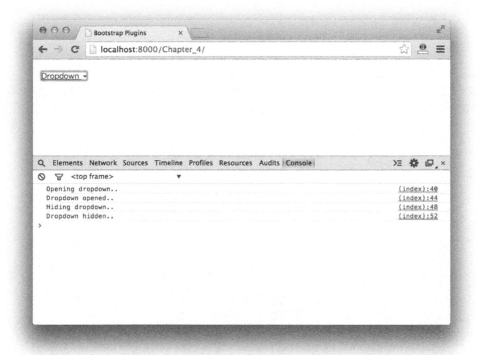

Figure 4.4. Clicking the handle again

Finally, `index.html` with the above events should look like this:

```
<!DOCTYPE html>
<html lang="en">
  <head>
    <meta charset="utf-8">
    <meta http-equiv="X-UA-Compatible" content="IE-edge">
    <meta name="viewport" content="width=device-width,
➥initial-scale=1">

    <title>Bootstrap Plugins</title>
    <link rel="stylesheet" type="text/css" href="css/bootstrap.css">

    <!--[if lt IE 9]>
      <script src="https://oss.maxcdn.com/libs/html5shiv/3.7.0/
➥html5shiv.js"></script>
      <script src="https://oss.maxcdn.com/libs/respond.js/1.4.2/
➥respond.min.js"></script>
    <![endif]-->
```

```html
    </head>
    <body>
        <div class="container">
            <div class="dropdown" id="myDropdown">
                <a class="myDropdownHandle" data-toggle="dropdown"
➥data-target="#" href="#">
                    Dropdown <span class="caret"></span>
                </a>
                <ul class="dropdown-menu">
                    <li><a href="#">Link 1</a></li>
                    <li><a href="#">Link 2</a></li>
                    <li><a href="#">Link 3</a></li>
                    <li><a href="#">Link 4</a></li>
                </ul>
            </div>
        </div>

    <script src="js/jquery.js"></script>
    <script src="js/bootstrap.js"></script>
    <script type="text/javascript">
        $(document).ready(function(){

            $('#myDropdown').on('show.bs.dropdown', function () {
                console.log("Opening dropdown..");
            });

            $('#myDropdown').on('shown.bs.dropdown', function () {
                console.log("Dropdown opened..");
            });

            $('#myDropdown').on('hide.bs.dropdown', function () {
                console.log("Hiding dropdown..");
            });

            $('#myDropdown').on('hidden.bs.dropdown', function () {
                console.log("Dropdown hidden..");
            });

        });
```

```
    </script>
  </body>
</html>
```

You will find these events extremely useful in situations where the links in the dropdown menu are dynamically populated with data from the server. In such cases, you can fire an Ajax request to the server on the `show.bs.dropdown` event and populate the dropdown menu before it is shown.

Alert Messages

Bootstrap comes with a very useful component for displaying alert messages in various sections of our website; you can use them for displaying a success message, a warning message, a failure message, or an information message. These messages can be annoying to visitors, hence they should have dismiss functionality added to give visitors the ability to hide them.

In this section, we'll create an alert message using Bootstrap and see how we can add dismiss functionality to it.

Here's the markup for a "success" alert message:

```
<div class="alert alert-success">
    Amount has been transferred successfully.
</div>
```

Every alert should have the `alert` class attached to it. It should also have an additional contextual class, such as `alert-success`. There are four self-explanatory contextual classes for alert messages:

1. `alert-success`
2. `alert-info`
3. `alert-danger`
4. `alert-warning`

The alert shown in the above code doesn't have a dismiss functionality, so it is always visible in the web page, as shown in Figure 4.5.

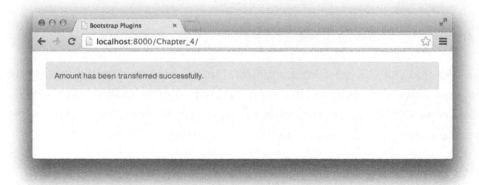

Figure 4.5. A regular alert message without dismiss functionality

The markup for a dismissable alert box, and what it looks like onscreen in Figure 4.6, is as follows:

```
<div class="alert alert-success alert-dismissable">
    <button type="button" class="close" data-dismiss="alert">
➥&times;</button>
    Amount has been transferred successfully.
</div>
```

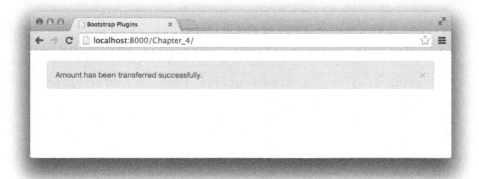

Figure 4.6. A dismissable alert box

To create a dismissable alert message, we need to add class `alert-dismissable` to the alert box. Next, we require a button that will close the alert message when clicked. The button should have `data-dismiss` attribute, which tells Bootstrap the component to dismiss when clicked. Bootstrap positions this button to the top-right position of the alert box with the help of the `close` class. This dismiss action on the close button is added by Bootstrap using JavaScript and captured using the `data-dismiss` attribute.

 Using Links Within an Alert

If you want to place a link within an alert, you need to add a class `alert-link` to the `a` element. This provides a matching color to link with respect to the alert box color:

```
<div class="alert alert-success alert-dismissable">
    <button type="button" class="close" data-dismiss=
➡"alert">&times;</button>
    Amount has been transferred successfully. Go to <a
➡href="#" class="alert-link">account page</a>.
</div>
```

Alert Messages with JavaScript

You can also dismiss an alert message using Bootstrap's `alert()` method in jQuery:

```
$(".alert").alert('close');
```

Alert messages have two events associated with them:

1. `close.bs.alert`: triggered just before closing the alert box

2. `closed.bs.alert`: triggered after the alert box is closed

Here's an example using the above events:

```
$('.alert').on('close.bs.alert', function () {
    console.log("Closing alert..");
});
```

```
$('.alert').on('closed.bs.alert', function () {
    console.log("Alert closed!");
});
```

Buttons

We saw how to create various types of buttons in the previous chapter. Here we'll see how we can use them in different situations and change their states using Bootstrap's JavaScript plugins.

Bootstrap buttons have two states: **active** and **inactive**. The active state has a class called `active`, but there's no class for the inactive state. Instead, you can create a simple button that toggles between these two states using the following markup:

```
<button type="button" class="btn btn-lg btn-default"
➡data-toggle="button">Toggle Me!</button>
```

In the code, I have created a large gray button using `btn`, `btn-lg`, and `btn-default` classes. It is currently in the inactive state. When the user clicks on it, Bootstrap will add an extra `active` class to the button.

When you click on the button, you'll see an inset-like style applied to it. On clicking again it reverts back to the original style, as shown in Figure 4.7. The attribute `data-toggle` with a value `button` helps in achieving this toggling functionality.

Toggle Me!

Toggle Me!

Figure 4.7. The two states of our button

Styling checkboxes and radio buttons with CSS can be tricky. Bootstrap has a way to redesign them; it makes a set of checkboxes or radio buttons into a set of Bootstrap buttons that are placed alongside each other. Let's go ahead and check out some sample markup, with the result shown in Figure 4.8:

```
<div class="btn-group" data-toggle="buttons">

    <label class="btn btn-default"
        <input type="checkbox"> Option 1
    </label>

    <label class="btn btn-default">
        <input type="checkbox"> Option 2
    </label>
```

```
    <label class="btn btn-default">
        <input type="checkbox"> Option 3
    </label>

</div>
```

| Option 1 | Option 2 | Option 3 |

Figure 4.8. Bootstrap Checkboxes

You can see in Figure 4.8 that Bootstrap has completely revamped the display of the checkboxes. They are now appearing as a group of Bootstrap buttons. Since they are checkboxes, I was able to check both Option 1 and Option 3. To create this group of checkboxes, you need a parent `div` with a class `btn-group`. It should also have an attribute `data-toggle` with a value of `buttons`. All the `checkbox`-type `input` elements should be wrapped inside `label` elements. These labels must have Bootstrap's button classes. In this case, I have opted for gray-colored buttons.

Multi-colored Checkboxes

You can create multi-colored buttons in the button group by mixing Bootstrap's button classes, such as `btn-primary`, `btn-info`, and so on.

You can also create a group of radio buttons in which only one button is selectable. Here's the markup with the result shown in Figure 4.9:

```
<div class="btn-group" data-toggle="buttons">

    <label class="btn btn-info">
        <input type="radio" name="options"> Option 1
    </label>

    <label class="btn btn-info">
        <input type="radio" name="options"> Option 2
    </label>
```

```
    <label class="btn btn-info">
        <input type="radio" name="options"> Option 3
    </label>

</div>
```

Figure 4.9. Bootstrap radio button

The only change in the markup is to modify the `type` attribute of the `input` element from `checkbox` to `radio`. Additionally, you have to logically group the radio buttons by applying a common `name` attribute value to all of them. In this case, I've also replaced `btn-default` to `btn-info` to change the color of the buttons from gray to light blue.

Buttons with JavaScript

Bootstrap comes with the `button()` method to toggle the state of the button through jQuery. You can use it in the following way:

```
$("mybutton").button('toggle');
```

You can also change the button to its `loading` state. In this state the button will remain disabled, but you need to define additional loading text using the `data-loading-text` attribute in the button element:

```
<button id="myLoadingButton" type="button" class="btn btn-primary"
➥data-loading-text="loading stuff...">Load data</button>
```

Let's change the state of the button to `loading` using jQuery when it's clicked:

```
$('#myLoadingButton').click(function () {
    $(this).button('loading');
});
```

The text on the button will change from "Load data" to "Loading stuff" when clicked. You can also reset the button state using the reset parameter in the button() method:

```
$("myLoadingButton").button('reset');
```

We also have an option to display different text when the loading is complete. We can do it using the data-complete-text attribute on the button and changing the state to complete using the .button('complete') method:

```
<button id="myLoadingButton" type="button" class="btn btn-primary"
➥data-complete-text="Completed!">Load data</button>
```

Managing Content

Managing content properly is extremely important for any website. If things become complicated then it's more likely that visitors won't return to your website. Bootstrap provides many JavaScript plugins that can help us organize and display our content. Let's have a look at some of them.

ScrollSpy

ScrollSpy is one of the most popular modern-day JavaScript plugins. It is widely used in websites that only have a single page. The plugin listens to scrolling within any DOM element and highlights a menu item in the navigation bar based upon the element's scroll position.

Basically, it is a two-component plugin; it consists of a navbar and a contents area. The contents area is divided into multiple sections, with each section having a unique ID. The navbar consists of only internal links with section IDs as the values of their href attribute. Once the user starts scrolling, the corresponding link in the navbar is highlighted as per the section that is currently on display.

Let's build a navbar first. Here's the markup:

```html
<nav id="navbarExample" class="navbar navbar-default"
➥role="navigation">
  <div class="container-fluid">
    <div class="navbar-header">
      <button class="navbar-toggle" type="button"
➥data-toggle="collapse" data-target=".navbarLinks">
        <span class="icon-bar"></span>
        <span class="icon-bar"></span>
        <span class="icon-bar"></span>
      </button>
      <a class="navbar-brand" href="#">SitePoint</a>
    </div>
    <div class="collapse navbar-collapse navbarLinks">
      <ul class="nav navbar-nav">
        <li class="active"><a href="#home">Home</a></li>
        <li class=""><a href="#about">About</a></li>
        <li class=""><a href="#contact">Contact Us</a></li>
        <li class=""><a href="#map">Map</a></li>
      </ul>
    </div>
  </div>
</nav>
```

The links in the navbar markup are all internal links to particular sections in the content.

The markup for the contents section is as follows:

```html
<div data-spy="scroll" data-target="#navbarExample" data-offset="0"
➥class="scrollspy-example">

    <h4 id="Home">Home</h4>
    <p>Lorem ipsum dolor sit amet, consectetur  ... </p>

    <h4 id="about">About</h4>
    <p>Lorem ipsum dolor sit amet, consectetur  ... </p>

    <h4 id="contact">Contact Us</h4>
    <p>Lorem ipsum dolor sit amet, consectetur  ... </p>

    <h4 id="map">Map</h4>
```

```
    <p>Lorem ipsum dolor sit amet, consectetur ... </p>

</div>
```

The contents section is composed of four pairs of <h4> and <p> tags. Each h4 element has a unique ID that matches with the internal links of the aforementioned navbar. To make the ScrollSpy work, you should add two custom data attributes to the content sections: `data-spy` and `data-target`. `data-spy` tells Bootstrap what the contents area is for the ScrollSpy plugin. It should have a value `scroll` to start listening to scrolling in this area. The `data-target` attribute tells which links it has to highlight. It should contains the ID of the parent of the nav element.

The `data-offset` attribute tells Bootstrap how many pixels to leave from the top before activating the ScrollSpy plugin. Sometimes, the navigation bar elements may be updated before we actually scroll to the actual element. This might happen if we've placed some additional HTML markup above the ScrollSpy area. This interferes with the area height calculation that is done internally by the plugin. We can use `data-offset` attribute and set the value as the height of the interfering element. Henceforth, the plugin will only start listening to the user's scrolling once the interfering element has been scrolled past.

Here's the full markup of **index.html** with ScrollSpy:

```html
<!DOCTYPE html>
<html lang="en">
  <head>
    <meta charset="utf-8">
    <meta http-equiv="X-UA-Compatible" content="IE=edge">
    <meta name="viewport" content="width=device-width,
➥initial-scale=1">

    <title>Bootstrap Plugins</title>
    <link rel="stylesheet" type="text/css" href="css/bootstrap.css">

    <!--[if lt IE 9]>
      <script src="https://oss.maxcdn.com/libs/html5shiv/
➥3.7.0/html5shiv.js"></script>
      <script src="https://oss.maxcdn.com/libs/respond.js/
➥1.4.2/respond.min.js"></script>
    <![endif]-->
```

```
    <style type="text/css">
        .scrollspy-example{
          position:relative;
          height:200px;
          margin-top:10px;
          overflow:auto}
    </style>

  </head>
  <body>
  <div class="container">
    <nav id="navbarExample" class="navbar navbar-default"
➥role="navigation">
      <div class="container-fluid">
        <div class="navbar-header">
          <button class="navbar-toggle" type="button"
➥data-toggle="collapse" data-target=".navbarLinks">
            <span class="icon-bar"></span>
            <span class="icon-bar"></span>
            <span class="icon-bar"></span>
          </button>
          <a class="navbar-brand" href="#">SitePoint</a>
        </div>
        <div class="collapse navbar-collapse navbarLinks">
          <ul class="nav navbar-nav">
            <li class="active"><a href="#home">Home</a></li>
            <li class=""><a href="#about">About</a></li>
            <li class=""><a href="#contact">Contact Us</a></li>
            <li class=""><a href="#map">Map</a></li>
          </ul>
        </div>
      </div>
    </nav>
    <div data-spy="scroll" data-target="#navbarExample"
➥data-offset="0" class="scrollspy-example">

      <h4 id="Home">Home</h4>
      <p>Lorem ipsum dolor sit amet, consectetur ... </p>

      <h4 id="about">About</h4>
      <p>Lorem ipsum dolor sit amet, consectetur ... </p>

      <h4 id="contact">Contact Us</h4>
      <p>Lorem ipsum dolor sit amet, consectetur ... </p>
```

```
        <h4 id="map">Map</h4>
        <p>Lorem ipsum dolor sit amet, consectetur ... </p>

    </div>
  </div>

    <script src="js/jquery.js"></script>
    <script src="js/bootstrap.js"></script>
  </body>
</html>
```

In Figure 4.10, you can see that I've scrolled down to the "About" section, and the "About" link is highlighted in the navbar.

Figure 4.10. Using ScrollSpy

ScrollSpy with JavaScript

Bootstrap has the `scrollspy()` method that takes optional parameters to customize the ScrollSpy plugin. You can set the target navbar's parent class through JavaScript by passing the appropriate options object as follows:

```
$('.scrollspy-example').scrollspy({ target: '#navbarExample' });
```

If you are passing options through JavaScript, you can ignore setting `data-*` attributes inside the element's markup.

Another important parameter that can be passed is the `refresh` string. If you've done DOM manipulations such as adding or deleting elements from the ScrollSpy area, you'll need to call the `scrollspy("refresh")` method. This will help ScrollSpy to recalculate the height of the scrollable area, which might have changed due to the addition and deletion of DOM elements:

```
$('.scrollspy-example').scrollspy("refresh");
```

ScrollSpy comes with only one custom event attached to it: `activate.bs.scrollspy`. It is fired whenever a new element is highlighted in the navbar. You can capture this event to do additional tasks, such as making Ajax requests to the server, performing extra calculations, and so on. Here's how we could use it:

```
$('#navbarExample').on('activate.bs.scrollspy', function () {
  console.log("New link highlighted!");
});
```

Tabs

In the previous chapter, we saw how to make a set of links look like tabs—but they weren't actually tabs! In this section, we are going to make some tab panes, put some dummy data into them, and make those tab panes respond to the corresponding tab links.

For tabs to work, we need Bootstrap's `nav-tabs` component and `tab-content` component. Let's create some `nav-tabs`:

```
<!-- Nav tabs -->
<ul class="nav nav-tabs">
  <li class="active"><a href="#home" data-toggle="tab">Home</a></li>
  <li><a href="#profile" data-toggle="tab">Profile</a></li>
  <li><a href="#messages" data-toggle="tab">Messages</a></li>
  <li><a href="#settings" data-toggle="tab">Settings</a></li>
</ul>
```

Each link in the `nav-tabs` component should have a `data-toggle` attribute with the value `tab`. This allows Bootstrap to map the click events to the corresponding tab pane. The `href` attribute in these links should contain the IDs of the corresponding tab panes.

Here's the markup for the tab panes:

```
<!-- Tab panes -->
<div class="tab-content">
    <div class="tab-pane active" id="home">
        <h3>The home</h3>
    </div>
    <div class="tab-pane" id="profile">
        <h3>The profile</h3>
    </div>
    <div class="tab-pane" id="messages">
        <h3>Messages central</h3>
    </div>
    <div class="tab-pane" id="settings">
        <h3>Setting panel</h3>
    </div>
</div>
```

To create tab panes, we need to first define a container for them. This container should have a class `tab-content`. For a tab pane, we need to create a new `div` element with the class `tab-pane`. These `tab-panes` should also have unique IDs, as these will be referenced to in the links of the `nav-tabs`. The number of `tab-panes` should be equal to the number of links present in `nav-tabs`. Adding the class `active` to a `li` element in `nav-tabs` and the corresponding `tab-pane` makes it the default tab.

That's it! You have a working tabs plugin. Go ahead and view it in the browser. The results are shown in Figure 4.11.

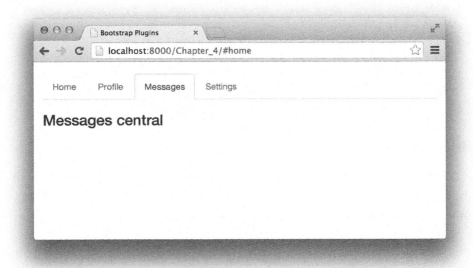

Figure 4.11. A working tab interface

 Adding a Fade Effect

Add the class `fade` to each `tab-pane` to apply a fading effect while switching between tabs. The first tab pane should also have a class `in` to properly apply a fading effect to the initial content:

```
<div class="tab-pane fade in active" id="home">
     <h3>The home</h3>
</div>
<div class="tab-pane fade" id="profile">
     <h3>The profile</h3>
</div>
```

Tabs with JavaScript

There are two JavaScript events associated with the tab plugin. These are:

1. `show.bs.tab`: this event is triggered on tab show, but before the new tab is opened

2. `shown.bs.tab`: the event is triggered after a tab is opened

Here's an example of how it's used:

```
$('.nav-tabs li a').on('show.bs.tab', function () {
    console.log("Opening tab");
});

$('.nav-tabs li a').on('shown.bs.tab', function () {
    console.log("Tab opened!");
});
```

Collapse

The **collapse** plugin is popularly known as an "accordion" plugin on the Web. It is a plugin that houses multiple vertically stacked tabs, but can open only one tab at a time. Figure 4.12 shows a screenshot of the collapse plugin.

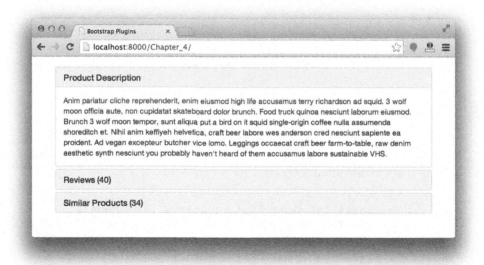

Figure 4.12. The collapse plugin

In Bootstrap, a collapse is created by housing multiple panel components together in a single container. We saw how to create a panel in the last chapter. We also know that a panel has two components: the `panel-heading` and `panel-body`.

To create a collapse, we need a group of panels housed inside a container. This container is created using a `div` element with the class `panel-group`. It should also have an ID associated with it.

```
<div class="panel-group" id="accordion">
</div>
```

We need to fill this container with different panels components that will serve as tabs. Let's create a single panel component inside this `panel-group`:

```
<div class="panel-group" id="accordion">

    <div class="panel panel-default">

        <div class="panel-heading">
            <h4 class="panel-title">
                <a data-toggle="collapse" data-parent="#accordion"
➥href="#collapseOne">
                Collapsible Group Item #1
                </a>
            </h4>
        </div>

        <div id="collapseOne" class="panel-collapse collapse in">
            <div class="panel-body">
            Lorem ipsum dolor sit ...
            </div>
        </div>

    </div>

</div>
```

Here, I have inserted the markup for a single panel component inside the panel group container. Every panel is divided into two parts: a `panel-heading` element and a `panel-body` element.

The `panel-heading` element contains an h4 element with an a element wraped within it. This combination of <h4> and <a> tags makes a tab in the collapse plugin. The h4 element should have a class `panel-title`. The a element should have three very important attributes: `data-toggle`, `data-parent`, and `href`. The `data-toggle` should represent what type of plugin it is. The `data-parent` element should contain the ID of the `panel-group` element. Finally, the `href` of such links should contain the ID of the parent element of `panel-body`.

Unlike normal panels where `panel-body` isn't wrapped inside any div, it is mandatory here to achieve the collapse effect. This wrapper element should have the classes `panel-collapse`, `collapse`, and `in`. The class `collapse` is used to hide the content whereas the combination of `collapse` and `in` displays the content. Hence, the first wrapper has both `collapse` and `in` classes and remaining all the wrappers should only have the `collapse` class. The class `panel-collapse` is used by Bootstrap's JavaScript to identify the wrapper.

Repeat the same markup for multiple tabs. The following markup shows a collapse plugin with three vertically stacked tabs, with the result shown in Figure 4.13:

```
<div class="panel-group" id="accordion">

    <!-- Panel 1 -->
    <div class="panel panel-default">
      <div class="panel-heading">
        <h4 class="panel-title">
          <a data-toggle="collapse" data-parent="#accordion"
➥href="#collapseOne">
            Collapsible Group Item #1
          </a>
        </h4>
      </div>
      <div id="collapseOne" class="panel-collapse collapse in">
          <div class="panel-body">
              Lorem ipsum dolor sit amet, consectetur ...
          </div>
      </div>
    </div>

    <!-- Panel 2 -->
    <div class="panel panel-default">
      <div class="panel-heading">
        <h4 class="panel-title">
          <a data-toggle="collapse" data-parent="#accordion"
➥href="#collapseTwo">
            Collapsible Group Item #2
          </a>
        </h4>
      </div>
      <div id="collapseTwo" class="panel-collapse collapse">
          <div class="panel-body">
              Lorem ipsum dolor sit amet, consectetur ...
          </div>
```

```
        </div>
      </div>

      <!-- Panel 3 -->
      <div class="panel panel-default">
        <div class="panel-heading">
          <h4 class="panel-title">
            <a data-toggle="collapse" data-parent="#accordion"
➥href="#collapseThree">
              Collapsible Group Item #3
            </a>
          </h4>
        </div>
        <div id="collapseThree" class="panel-collapse collapse">
          <div class="panel-body">
              Lorem ipsum dolor sit amet, consectetur ...
          </div>
        </div>
      </div>
    </div>
```

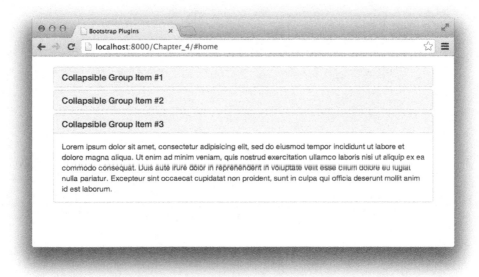

Figure 4.13. Final collapse plugin

Collapse with JavaScript

Bootstrap provides the `collapse()` method for changing the default behavior of the collapse plugin. By default, only one tab can be opened at a time. We can override this behavior by passing the custom `options` object to the above method. Let's do that.

In the previous collapse plugin's markup we had added a class `collapse` to all the `panel-body` wrappers. Let's select this class and call the `collapse()` method on it:

```
$('.collapse').collapse({
        toggle: false
});
```

In the snippet, I have passed an anonymous object that has a property `toggle` with a value set to `false`. This will force all the tabs to stay open when other tabs are opening. Go ahead and try it yourself.

As shown in Figure 4.14, you can see all the tabs are opened simultaneously.

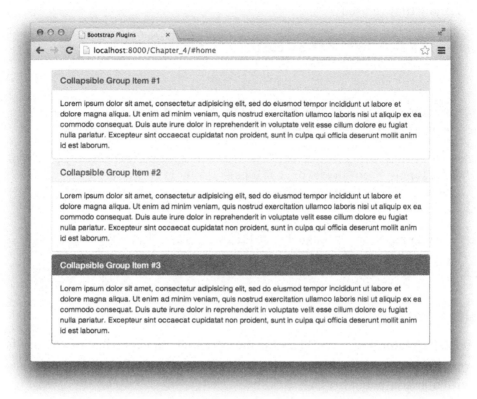

Figure 4.14. All tabs open in our collapse

You also have option to pass various predefined strings to the `collapse()` method:

1. `collapse('toggle')`: toggles the tab from one state to another

2. `collapse('show')`: opens a tab

3. `collapse('hide')`: closes a tab

Bootstrap also comes with four custom events attached to the collapse plugin:

1. `show.bs.collapse`: fired just before opening the tab

2. `shown.bs.collapse`: fired after the tab is opened

3. `hide.bs.collapse`: fired just before closing the tab

4. `hidden.bs.collapse`: fired after the tab is closed

Here's how they're used:

```
$('.collapse').on('show.bs.collapse', function () {
    console.log('Opening tab..');
});

$('.collapse').on('shown.bs.collapse', function () {
    console.log('Tab opened.');
});

$('.collapse').on('hide.bs.collapse', function () {
    console.log('Hiding tab..');
});

$('.collapse').on('hidden.bs.collapse', function () {
    console.log('Tab hidden');
});
```

Tooltip

A Bootstrap **tooltip** is a small floating message that appears when the mouse is hovered over a component in a website. It is generally used to display help text for a particular component.

Bootstrap's tooltip is made using CSS and triggered through JavaScript. It's extremely lightweight compared to many other tooltip plugins available today. There are also easy customization options to position the tooltip with respect to its parent component (top, bottom, right, and left). To use a tooltip, we have to define some custom data-* attributes.

Let's build a demo tooltip on a button component:

```
<button type="button" class="btn btn-default" data-toggle="tooltip"
➡data-placement="bottom" title="I am a Bootstrap button">Who am I?
➡</button>
```

You need to add a data-toggle attribute with the value tooltip, a title attribute containing the text that you want to display in the tooltip, and a data-placement attribute. The data-placement attribute accepts one of the following four values: top, bottom, left, and right. As its name suggests, the data-placement attribute defines the position of the tooltip with respect to its parent component.

Let's go ahead and view this button in a browser. You'll see that it fails to work; there's no tooltip when the mouse is hovered on the button. For performance reasons, in Bootstrap tooltips need to be initialized manually through jQuery. So let's go ahead and add the following script, after all the `<script>` tags in the body:

```
<script type="text/javascript">
  $(document).ready(function(){
    $('.tooltipButton').tooltip();
  });
</script>
```

In this code we have used the `tooltipButton` class as the selector. Hence, we need to add this class to the button for the tooltip to work.

We also need to modify the HTML code of the button and add the class `tooltipButton` to it:

```
<button type="button" class="btn btn-default tooltipButton"
➥data-toggle="tooltip" data-placement="bottom"
➥title="I am a Bootstrap button">Who am I?</button>
```

Refresh the web page and a tooltip should appear, as shown in Figure 4.15.

Figure 4.15. A tooltip

Tooltip with JavaScript

We have just seen that we need to call the `tooltip()` method to make the tooltip function. Here, we'll see how we can customize the tooltip plugin by passing various options through this function.

The method takes an object containing various optional properties for changing the general behavior of atooltip:

```
var options = {
    animation : true;
};

$(".tooltipButton").tooltip(options);
```

In the code, I have defined a JavaScript object called `options`. I've set the property `animation` to `true` so that the tooltip gets a fading effect whenever its displayed. Finally, I have passed this object to the `tooltip()` method.

Other properties that can be passed are:

- html: This property takes a Boolean value. If it is set to true then the content that is present inside the title attribute will be parsed as HTML. Otherwise, it will be displayed as-is.

- placement: This property takes five string values: top, bottom, left, right, and auto. It defines the position of thetooltip with respect to the component. If set to auto, the tooltip will be oriented automatically.

- selector: This is a special option available from Bootstrap. If you have called the tooltip() method on a parent container, you might like to filter the child elements on which this tooltip should work, and you can do that with this option. You can provide values such as a, a[href='hello.html'] or button[class='tooltipbuttons'].

- title: If you didn't use the custom attribute data-title in the HTML markup, you can pass the tooltip title through this option. This takes a string value, such as title: "This is a button".

- trigger: All the tooltips are shown by hovering over the component. Use this option to override the default behavior. Values that this option can take are: click, focus, hover, and manual. You can also combine these values separated by a space; for example click hover, hover focus, and so on.

- delay: If you want to avoid having the tooltip appear immediately, use this property to set a delay amount (in milliseconds).

- container: Use this property to append a tooltip to specific elements such as body. This will prevent the tooltip from floating away from the triggering element during a window resize.

Apart from accepting an options object, the tooltip() method also accepts several predefined string values. These strings are mapped to the custom behavior of the tooltip; for example:

```
$('.tooltipButton').tooltip('show');
```

Passing the string "show"will make the tooltip appear. Possible string values are:

1. "show": shows the tooltip

2. "hide": hides the tooltip

3. "toggle": toggles the state of the tooltip (if a tooltip is currently hidden this will show it, and vice versa)

4. "destroy": this string hides and destroys the tooltip related to a particular element; once destroyed, the associated tooltip cannot be used again

Just like other Bootstrap plugins, tooltip also comes with custom events that can be captured to perform extra tasks. These events are:

1. show.bs.tooltip: this event is fired before the tooltip is visible

2. shown.bs.tooltip: this event is fired after the tooltip is visible

3. hide.bs.tooltip: fired before the tooltip is hidden

4. hidden.bs.tooltip: fired after the tooltip is hidden

Here's how you'd use them:

```
$('.tooltipButton').on('show.bs.tooltip', function () {
  console.log("Showing tooltip..");
});

$('.tooltipButton').on('shown.bs.tooltip', function () {
  console.log("Tooltip shown.");
});

$('.tooltipButton').on('hide.bs.tooltip', function () {
  console.log("Hiding tooltip..");
});
```

```
$('.tooltipButton').on('hidden.bs.tooltip', function () {
  console.log("Tooltip hidden.");
});
```

Popovers

Popovers are another useful plugin that are comparable to tooltips. The difference is that popovers are larger and more stylish than tooltips, as shown in Figure 4.16. They look very similar to the popovers in Apple iBooks' dictionary feature.

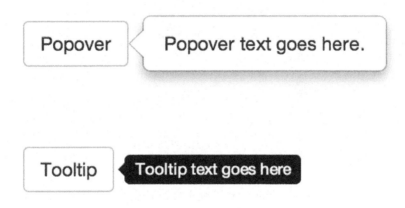

Figure 4.16. Popovers versus tooltips

You can place more content in a popover than a tooltip. It is recommended to use popovers instead of tooltips when you have more HTML content or textual content to display.

Let's trigger a popover to activate on the click event of a button. The markup to do this is:

```
<button type="button" class="btn btn-danger" data-toggle="popover"
➥data-placement="bottom" data-content="Lorem Ipsum Donor."
➥title="This is a demo popover">
  Click Me!
</button>
```

There are a few custom data-* attributes that are necessary for the popover plugin to function. These are similar to the custom attributes used in tooltips. The data-toggle attribute directs what to trigger when an action is performed on this button. The data-placement attribute specifies the position of the popover. The data-content attribute should contain the content you want to convey in the popover. Finally, set the title attribute to append a header to the plugin.

Just like tooltips, popovers should also be manually initiated. You can use the following script:

```
<script type="text/javascript"
  $(document).ready(function(){
      $('.popoverButton').popover();
  });
</script>
```

As the selector in this code is a class, we need to add the popoverButton class to the button. The results are shown in Figure 4.17.

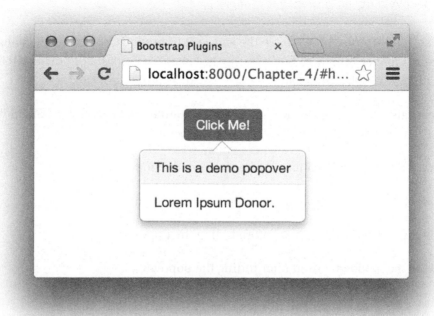

Figure 4.17. Popover

Popovers with JavaScript

Bootstrap provides the `popover()` method for customizing the default behavior of the popover plugin. It accepts an options object, just like the tooltip plugin. All the options properties available to the tooltip plugin discussed earlier also apply to the popover plugin.

For example:

```
var options = {
    animation: true,
    placement: "right"
};

$('.popoverButton').popover(options);
```

The popover plugin also accepts a set of predefined strings that are mapped to certain behaviors of a popover; for instance:

```
$('.popoverButton').popover("show");
```

Just like a tooltip plugin, we have the same set of predefined strings to change the state of a popover plugin. When passing the "show" string, the popover will be visible. Other available strings are: "hide", "toggle" and "destroy".

Popovers also come with custom events very similar to the events of the tooltip plugin. The events associated with popovers are:

1. show.bs.popover: fired just before showing the popover

2. shown.bs.popover: fired after the popover is shown

3. hide.bs.popover: fired just before hiding the popover

4. hidden.bs.popover: fired after hiding the popover

Usage is similar to the tooltip plugin:

```
$('.popoverButton').on('show.bs.popover', function () {
    console.log("Opening popover..");
});

$('.popoverButton').on('shown.bs.popover', function () {
    console.log("Popover opened.");
});

$('.popoverButton').on('hide.bs.popover', function () {
    console.log("Hiding popover..");
});

$('.popoverButton').on('hidden.bs.popover', function () {
    console.log("Popover hidden.");
});
```

Getting Fancy

In this section, we will be discussing two very important plugins: **carousel** and **modal**.

Carousel is a responsive slideshow plugin and modal is a lightbox-like plugin. Each one lets you showcase your content in a fancy way.

Carousel

Slideshows are very popular, and can be used for news, ecommerce, and video sharing sites, for instance. This type of feature is used to showcase the most popular items on the website in a well-organized, attractive slideshow. Building such slideshows can be time-consuming, however, and these features can also be prone to bugs. In this section, we'll see how to use Bootstrap's **carousel** plugin to build beautiful responsive slideshows.

The markup for creating a carousel is as follows:

```
<div id="bestCarsCarousel" class="carousel slide"
➥data-ride="carousel">

    <!-- Indicators -->
    <ol class="carousel-indicators">
        <li data-target="#bestCarsCarousel" data-slide-to="0"
➥class="active"></li>
        <li data-target="#bestCarsCarousel" data-slide-to="1"></li>
        <li data-target="#bestCarsCarousel" data-slide-to="2"></li>
    </ol>

    <!-- Wrapper for slides -->
    <div class="carousel-inner">
        <div class="item active">
            <img src="images/car1.jpg">
            <div class="carousel-caption">
                <h3>Car 1</h3>
                <p>Lorem ipsum dolor sit amet, consectetur ...</p>
            </div>
        </div>

        <div class="item">
            <img src="images/car2.jpg">
            <div class="carousel-caption">
                <h3>Car 2</h3>
                <p>Lorem ipsum dolor sit amet, consectetur ...</p>
            </div>
        </div>

        <div class="item">
            <img src="images/car3.jpg">
            <div class="carousel-caption" >
                <h3>Car 3</h3>
```

```
                    <p>Lorem ipsum dolor sit amet, consectetur ...</p>
                </div>
            </div>
        </div>

        <!-- Controls -->
        <a class="left carousel-control" href="#bestCarsCarousel"
➥data-slide="prev">
            <span class="glyphicon glyphicon-chevron-left"></span>
        </a>
        <a class="right carousel-control" href="#bestCarsCarousel"
➥data-slide="next">
            <span class="glyphicon glyphicon-chevron-right"></span>
        </a>
    </div>
```

As seen in the code, the main wrapper container for our carousel should have the classes `carousel` and `slide`. The class `slide` is used to give a sliding effect to each slide in the carousel. It should also have a custom attribute `data-ride`, which tells Bootstrap to start the sliding effect as soon as the page loads. Without this attribute the slides will fail to change automatically until you've done so manually the first time.

Every carousel plugin has three subsections in it: indicators, body, and controls.

To create a carousel Indicator, you have to define an ordered list with a class of `carousel-indicators`. The number of `li` elements in it depends on the number of slides you want to have. Each `li` element should have a `data-target` attribute containing the ID of the carousel container. It should also have a `data-slide-to` attribute containing the sequence number of the particular slide it will point to.

Next, we build the heart of the carousel, the slides. First, we create a wrapper element for all the slides. This will be a `div` with the class `carousel-inner`. Each slide is defined by a `div` element that has a class `item`. Every item must have a representing image and optional textual data. This image will be used as a background for that particular slide item. For each image we can add related captions and some additional textual data. These captions are wrapped by a `div` element that has a class `carousel-caption`. The caption can be inserted using any one of the HTML heading tags: `<h1>`, `<h2>`, `<h3>`, and so on. For related text you can use `<p>` tags.

Repeat the same `item` markup for each slide. After you're done with creating all the slides, we'll build a controls section for navigating carousel content.

The carousel controls are constructed using `<a>` tags with a class `carousel-control` and one of the directional classes such as `left` or `right`. The `href` attribute of these links should contain the ID of the carousel wrapper. Once the controls are formed, we insert left and right symbols in them. These symbols are glyphicons.

It's time to check the carousel in the browser, shown in Figure 4.18.

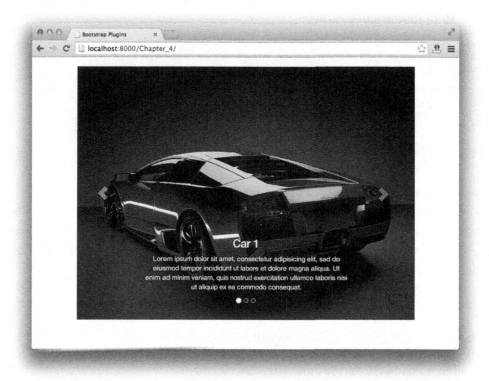

Figure 4.18. A carousel of cars

Amazing, no? We have created a powerful responsive slideshow without writing a single piece of JavaScript or CSS.

 Carousels and Older Versions of IE

Though Bootstrap may be compatible with IE8 and above, the carousel is not fully compatible. The sliding effect will fail to work in CSS3-incompatible browsers such as IE8 and I9. The carousel indicators will appear as squares in these browsers, rather than being circular.

Carousel with JavaScript

Bootstrap has the `carousel()` method for calling carousels through JavaScript. You can use this method to pass customized options to change the default behavior of a carousel.

There are only three JavaScript options available for carousel: `interval`, `pause`, and `wrap`. Here they are in the code:

```
var options = {
    interval: 7000,
    pause: 'hover',
    wrap: true
};

$('#bestCarsCarousel').carousel(options);
```

The `interval` property is used to specify the time duration between each slide. The `pause` option takes only one value `hover`, which tells Bootstrap to stop carousel sliding on mouse hover. The `wrap` option takes Boolean values to set the cycling of carousel to on or off. If set to `true`, the carousel will start sliding to the first slide after displaying the last slide and this will continue.

Other parameters that can also be passed to the `carousel()` method include:

1. `cycle`: to enable cycling functionality of a carousel

2. `pause`: to pause the slideshow from JavaScript

3. `number`: to specify the time duration between two slides

4. `prev`: to change the slide to the previous slide

5. `next`: to change the slide to the next slide

The carousel plugin comes with two custom events:

1. `slide.bs.carousel`: fired before the slide is changed

2. `slid.bs.carousel`: fired after the slide has changed

Here's how to use them:

```javascript
$('#bestCarsCarousel').on('slide.bs.carousel', function () {
    console.log("Changing slide..");
});

$('#bestCarsCarousel').on('slid.bs.carousel', function () {
    console.log("Slide changed.");
});
```

Modals

Modals are HTML elements that are hidden in a web page, sliding down from the top of the screen when triggered. It is one of the best plugins to use to display dialog prompts, such as alert and confirm dialogs. You can also use it to showcase a larger version of an image, display a long list of terms and conditions, or to display sign-up/login forms.

With Bootstrap 3, modals have become responsive. This means that they look good and operate well even on smaller screens. Let's go ahead and create a modal:

```html
<div class="modal fade" id="myModal">

    <div class="modal-dialog">

        <div class="modal-content">

            <!-- Modal Header -->
            <div class="modal-header">
                <button type="button" class="close"
 data-dismiss="modal">&times;</button>
                <h4 class="modal-title">Welcome Back!</h4>
            </div>

            <!-- Modal Body -->
            <div class="modal-body">
                <h1>Hello Readers!</h1>
            </div>

            <!-- Modal Footer -->
            <div class="modal-footer">
```

```
                  <button type="button" class="btn btn-default"
➥data-dismiss="modal">Close</button>
                  <button type="button" class="btn btn-primary">
➥Save changes</button>
            </div>

        </div>
    </div>
</div>
```

Every modal should have a container with the class `modal`. To give a fading effect
to the modal we need to add the class `fade` as well to the same container. Next, we
define a `div` element that has a class `modal-dialog`. This is responsible for con-
trolling the size of the modal. By default, it's resized as per the size of the screen.
Shortly we'll see how to change the size of the modal by adding some additional
classes to `modal-dialog`. Inside the modal dialog, we'll create a wrapper element
that wraps various subsections of a modal. This wrapper element should have a
class called `modal-content`.

The subsections to the modal are the header, body and footer. The header and
footer part are optional. To create a modal header, you need a `div` element with
class `modal-header`. Inside it you can put a modal title and a modal dismiss icon.
The modal title is given using an `h4` element with class `modal-title`. The dismiss
icon here is a multiplication (x) symbol that is wrapped around a `button` element.
This button should have the class `close` so that it is aligned to the top-right corner
of the modal header. Adding a `data-dismiss` attribute enables the button to close
the modal when clicked.

For the body, we need a `div` with the class `modal-body`. You can put almost any
content inside this element. You can even use Bootstrap's grid system to organize
content properly inside it.

Finally, for creating a modal footer, we define a `div` element that has a class `modal-
footer`. The content inside a modal footer are right-aligned by default.

If you check the previous modal code snippet inside a browser, you will find
nothing; modals are hidden in nature. You have to create a handle to trigger it:

```
<button class="btn btn-primary btn-lg" data-toggle="modal"
➥data-target="#myModal">
    Launch modal
  </button>
```

In this code, I've used a button component to trigger the modal. It should have a `data-target` attribute to tell Bootstrap which modal to trigger as there can be multiple modals in a website. We also need the `data-toggle` attribute defined to determine what to trigger when clicked.

Now we are all set to use our modal. Go ahead and click on the button to see a modal fading within the browser, as depicted in Figure 4.19.

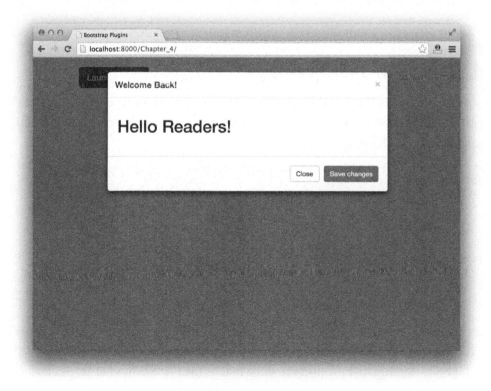

Figure 4.19. Our modal

Modal Placement

The modal markup has to be placed in the top-level position in the document to prevent conflict with other components. Yet there's no restriction when placing the modal handle. It can be placed anywhere in the document.

Modals come in three widths: large, default, and small. These can be really helpful for fitting the content properly in the modal dialog.

If no additional class is provided to `modal-dialog`, it will appear in the default width of 600p. To make the modal large or small, you need to add one of these classes to the `modal-dialog` element:

- `modal-lg`: for a large modal of width 900px

- `modal-sm`: for a small modal of width 300px

Modals with JavaScript

Bootstrap provides the `modal()` method to trigger a modal through JavaScript. This method also accepts an options object containing various properties for customizing the default behavior of a modal:

```
var options = {
    backdrop: true,
    keyboard: false,
    show: true,
    remote: false
}

$("#myModal").modal(options);
```

The `backdrop` propertiy accepts Boolean values or the string value "`static`". When a modal is launched, a dark transparent backdrop appears by default behind the modal body. Setting this property to `true` makes the backdrop visible. Set it to `false` and the backdrop disappears. When set to "`static`" , the modal won't close when there's a click anywhere outside the modal body.

The `keyboard` property is used to enable or disable escape key functionality from the keyboard. When set to false, the **Esc** key won't close the modal.

The show property is used to toggle the visibility of the modal through JavaScript. When set to true, the modal will appear automatically without requiring a click on any handle element.

The a element, which may be used as a modal handle element, can comprise an attribute href containing a link. The Bootstrap modal has an option to load this link inside its modal-body element when clicked on the handle. This feature is turned off by default. If you want to use this feature and load the link inside the modal-body, set the remote property to true.

Events associated with Bootstrap modal include:

1. show.bs.modal: fired just before opening the modal
2. shown.bs.modal: fired after the modal is open
3. hide.bs.modal: fired just before hiding the modal
4. hidden.bs.modal: fired after the modal is hidden
5. loaded.bs.modal: fired after the remote content is loaded

Here's how they are used:

```
$('#myModal').on('show.bs.modal', function () {
    console.log("Opening Modal..");
});

$('#myModal').on('shown.bs.modal', function () {
    console.log("Modal opened.");
});

$('#myModal').on('hide.bs.modal', function () {
    console.log("Hiding Modal..");
});

$('#myModal').on('hidden.bs.modal', function () {
    console.log("Modal hidden.");
});
```

Summary

Through this chapter, we have learned how to use many of the popular Bootstrap JavaScript plugins. We have also learned how to customize them by setting custom data-* attributes and through JavaScript. When working with Bootstrap, you should always make use of the built-in plugins whenever possible and avoid writing custom plugins.

Chapter 5

Diving Deep: Customizing Bootstrap

Imagine a Web where all the websites built with Bootstrap look and feel the same. Boring, right? Fortunately, we have the power to change the default styles of any framework we work with.

Many of Bootstrap's components and plugins have their own default styles. In order to give them a personal touch, you need to replace their CSS rules and define your own.

In the first chapter, I shared with you some of the popular websites built on Bootstrap. They have all customized Bootstrap's CSS to make their templates look unique and beautiful.

In this chapter, we'll discuss the various methods we can use to completely customize Bootstrap's default styles, and analyze which method is more preferable and why. Finally, we will try to understand how Bootstrap's CSS was written to make it a highly responsive framework.

Customizing Bootstrap Stylesheets

You can customize Bootstrap in various ways. In this section, we'll see customization through static CSS files and through Less files.

What's Less?

Less[1] is a CSS preprocessor that extends CSS capabilities, adding programming features such as variables, mixins, functions, and so on. It keeps CSS modular, maintainable, and extendible. Less files are compiled to generate CSS files that you can then use in your projects.

If you work with Ruby, Sass[2] is an alternative to Less. It is also a CSS preprocessor that Bootstrap supports; however, we won't be covering Sass customizations in this book.

The stylesheets that come with Bootstrap's default package are normal CSS files. If you open the static CSS files using a text editor, you'll find lots of selectors and their associated CSS properties. You may be tempted to directly change CSS properties and their values in these files to save time, but I would strongly advise against it.

There are many disadvantages of directly modifying the CSS files. Some of the important ones are:

- The changes are irreversible. You won't remember the CSS properties and their values that were present originally, so you'll be unable to revert back to the original Bootstrap style.

- Any changes made by you to one selector may break down the responsiveness of Bootstrap.

- Debugging becomes very difficult; you need to understand the CSS inheritance chain to reach the parent selector.

Before we jump into customization, let's first set up the project that will be used in this chapter. As always, we'll be using the project created in Chapter 1, Boot-

---

[1] http://lesscss.org

[2] http://sass-lang.com

strap_demos. Copy all the contents into a new folder named **Chapter_5**. Open **index.html** and change the title of the page to "Customizing Bootstrap". Now remove the <h1> tag from the body.

Customizing Bootstrap Using CSS

This type of customization is generally known as **overriding the default CSS**. We effectively overwrite some of Bootstrap's CSS properties with different values of our own.

First, we create a new file called **app.css** (or whatever you wish) inside the **/css** folder. Then we open **index.html** and link to the new CSS file. The link to this new CSS file should be included just below the link to Bootstrap's CSS file:

```
<link rel="stylesheet" type="text/css" href="css/bootstrap.css">
<link rel="stylesheet" type="text/css" href="css/app.css">
```

Let's add a Bootstrap button, shown in Figure 5.1. We'll use that to show how to make some changes to its default design:

```
<div class="container">
    <a href="#" class="btn btn-primary btn-lg">Big Fat Button</a>
</div>
```

Figure 5.1. Our default button

Here's what we'll now do to customize this button:

- remove the rounded corners from this button
- alter the padding amount
- tweak the font size
- change the background color

Let's inspect the button using a developer tool. We'll use Chrome, as shown in Figure 5.2, but you can use any similar tool of your choice, such as Firebug in Firefox. The properties such as padding, font-size, and border-radius come from the class btn, whereas the property background is applied through the class btn-primary. To modify them, we'll need to override the properties using the same selectors in our CSS file, app.css.

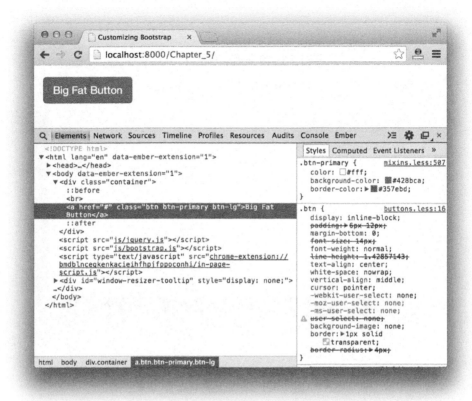

Figure 5.2. Inspecting our button in Chrome's developer tool

Open **app.css** and add the following CSS:

```css
.btn{
    border-radius: 0;
    padding: 5px 10px;
    font-size: 16px;
}

.btn-primary{
    background: #63AEF0;
}
```

If we refresh our page, our button should now look like Figure 5.3.

Figure 5.3. A customized button

Note that we have used the Bootstrap classes `btn` and `btn-primary` to override the CSS styles. Henceforth, whenever you use Bootstrap's button component it will have a changed style that looks like Figure 5.3. To revert back to the original style, we simply remove the CSS styles from the **app.css** file.

If you want to change the style of only a particular button in your web page, instead of targeting Bootstrap's selectors, use IDs to apply a CSS change.

Customizing Bootstrap Using Less

If you are a Less developer you will love this section, as there are plenty of options for working with Less to customize Bootstrap. There's a Less file for every Bootstrap component to change their properties easily. To access all the Less files, you need to download a particular version of Bootstrap. Go to http://getbootstrap.com/getting-started/ and select **Download Source**. This source package contains both compiled and raw **.less** files.

The Less files are located inside the folder called **less**. Here, you will find many **.less** files named as per Bootstrap's components. All the CSS properties and values related to a particular component are present inside the corresponding **.less** file. You will also find a file named **bootstrap.less**, which is the main **.less** file. It imports all the **.less** files present inside that folder. You need to compile only this file to generate a customized Bootstrap stylesheet. Let's categorize all the files inside this folder.

Bootstrap's Variables and the Mixins

All the variables and mixins used in Bootstrap are present inside two distinct files:

1. **variables.less** contains all standard colors used in Bootstrap, default responsive width values, default padding values, and margin values. If you want to make any such changes you need to deal with this file.

2. **mixins.less** contains mixins to generate vendor prefixes and dynamically calculate widths of grids, placeholders, button sizes, and so on.

Reset Files

There are two reset files to clear browser defaults:

1. **normalize.less** clears many browser defaults like font family, font sizes, paddings and margins, heading tags defaults, styles of form elements, and so on.

2. **print.less** contains media queries for print support.

Core Files

There are seven core **.less** files:

- **scaffolding.less** contains all the helper classes for images (such as `.img-responsive` and `.img-circle`), styles for various states of link elements, horizontal rules, styles for screen readers, and so on.

- **type.less** is a typography file that contains various styling for heading tags, paragraph tags, and other content-related helper classes such as `.lead`, `.text-muted`, and so forth.

- **code.less** contains CSS properties for styling any code presented on the web page.

- **grid.less** is concerned with all the CSS values applied on the Bootstrap grid system.

- **tables.less** has styles for decorating the `<table>` element. It also defines various helper classes for tables such as `.table-condensed`, `.table-bordered`, and so on.

- **forms.less** beautifies form elements such as text fields, legends, checkboxes, radio buttons, and so forth.

- **buttons.less** contains styles for styling various types of Bootstrap buttons. All the button-related classes are defined here.

Component Files

There are 21 component files in Bootstrap. Each component covered in the previous chapter has its own **.less** file. All the CSS definitions related to a component can be found in its **.less file.**

- **component-animations.less**
- **glyphicons.less**
- **dropdowns.less**
- **button-groups.less**
- **input-groups.less**
- **navs.less**
- **navbar.less**
- **breadcrumbs.less**
- **pagination**.less
- **pager.less**
- **labels.less**
- **badges.less**
- **jumbotron.less**
- **thumbnails.less**
- **alerts.less**
- **progress-bars.less**
- **media.less**
- **list-group.less**
- **panels**.less

- wells.less
- close.less

There's an additional file in this list that is not actually a component in itself, `close.less`. It contains the CSS rules for the dismiss button used in modals, alerts, and other elements to close this particular component.

Plugin Files

There are four **.less** files that define the CSS styles of JavaScript plugins triggered or created using Bootstrap's markup:

- modals.less
- tooltip.less
- popovers.less
- carousel.less

Utility Files

Finally, we have two utility files in Bootstrap:

- utilities.less
- responsive-utilities.less

These files define classes that help us to better organize the Bootstrap components. They have helpful classes such as `.clearfix` to clear a component from all the elements present around it, and `.hide` and `.show` to toggle visibility of components, for example. **responsive-utilities.less** contains visibility utilities such as `.visible-lg` and `.hidden-sm`.

Overriding Styles Using Less

Let's use Less to override the style of a modal. We will customize `modals.less` to apply a flat (metro-style) design, remove the rounded corners, and reduce the shadow applied to it. We will also change the background color and text color of the modal. Let's open **modals.less** and make these changes.

The rounded corners to the modal are applied through the class `modal-content`. Let's find this selector in **modals.less**. It should look like this:

```
// Actual modal
.modal-content {
  position: relative;
  background-color: @modal-content-bg;
  border: 1px solid @modal-content-fallback-border-color;
➥//old browsers fallback (ie8 etc)
  border: 1px solid @modal-content-border-color;
  border-radius: @border-radius-large;
  .box-shadow(0 3px 9px rgba(0,0,0,.5));
  background-clip: padding-box;
  // Remove focus outline from opened modal
  outline: 0;
}
```

From the code, we can see the rounded corners come from the property `border-radius` whose value is a Less variable initialized in **variables.less**. Let's comment out this line to remove rounded corners:

```
// Actual modal
.modal-content {
  position: relative;
  background-color: @modal-content-bg;
  border: 1px solid @modal-content-fallback-border-color;
➥//old browsers fallback (ie8 etc)
  border: 1px solid @modal-content-border-color;
//  border-radius: @border-radius-large;
  .box-shadow(0 3px 9px rgba(0,0,0,.5));
  background-clip: padding-box;
  // Remove focus outline from opened modal
  outline: 0;
}
```

Now, we have to reduce the amount of shadow. Analyzing the code, we can see that the `.box-shdow()` mixin is responsible for producing the shadow property in CSS. This mixin is defined in the **mixins.less** file, and the shadow values are passed as a value to this mixin. Let's change this value as per our requirement. The amount of shadow is defined by the third number in the value, which is passed as the argument—it's 9px currently. Let's reduce this number to 2px. Hence, our selector should now look like this:

```
// Actual modal
.modal-content {
  position: relative;
  background-color: @modal-content-bg;
  border: 1px solid @modal-content-fallback-border-color;
➥//old browsers fallback (ie8 etc)
  border: 1px solid @modal-content-border-color;
  border-radius: @border-radius-large;
  .box-shadow(0 3px 2px rgba(0,0,0,.5));
  background-clip: padding-box;
  // Remove focus outline from opened modal
  outline: 0;
}
```

We also need to change the box-shadow value in one of the media queries, which
overrides the previous changes. We'll learn about media queries soon. But for now,
you need to understand that Bootstrap has different CSS rules for devices of unique
sizes. So let's go ahead and find the following media query in **modals.less**:

```
// Scale up the modal
@media (min-width: @screen-sm-min) {
  // Automatically set modal's width for larger viewports
  .modal-dialog {
    width: @modal-md;
    margin: 30px auto;
  }
  .modal-content {
    .box-shadow(0 5px 15px rgba(0,0,0,.5));
  }

  // Modal sizes
  .modal-sm { width: @modal-sm; }
}
```

Let's pass the new box-shadow value to the .box-shadow() mixin in this media
query:

```
// Scale up the modal
@media (min-width: @screen-sm-min) {
  // Automatically set modal's width for larger viewports
  .modal-dialog {
    width: @modal-md;
```

```
    margin: 30px auto;
  }
  .modal-content {
    .box-shadow(0 5px 2px rgba(0,0,0,.5));
  }

  // Modal sizes
  .modal-sm { width: @modal-sm; }
}
```

Let's now change the modal's background color. We'll use a predefined variable @brand-info from **variables.less** as the background color of the modal. This variable is initialized to #5bc0de, which is a light blue color. For the text color, let's use the variable @body-bg, which is set to #fff in the same file. The modified modal-content selector should now look like:

```
// Actual modal
.modal-content {
  position: relative;
  background-color: @modal-content-bg;
  border: 1px solid @modal-content-fallback-border-color;
➥//old browsers fallback (ie8 etc)
  border: 1px solid @modal-content-border-color;
  border-radius: @border-radius-large;
  .box-shadow(0 3px 9px rgba(0,0,0,.5));
  background-clip: padding-box;
  // Remove focus outline from opened modal
  outline: 0;

  background: @brand-info;
  color: @body-bg;

}
```

We have made all the customizations planned, but let's make one final change to the modal-backdrop selector. modal-backdrop is a transparent layer that appears behind the modal-content whenever the modal component is triggered.

Let's change the background color of this modal-background from black to white:

```less
// Modal background
.modal-backdrop {
  position: fixed;
  top: 0;
  right: 0;
  bottom: 0;
  left: 0;
  z-index: @zindex-modal-background;
  background-color: @body-bg;
  // Fade for backdrop
  &.fade { .opacity(0); }
  &.in { .opacity(@modal-backdrop-opacity); }
}
```

Finally, we are done with all the customization. It's time to compile the **bootstrap.less** file that imports **modals.less**. Once the **.less** file is compiled to generate **bootstrap.css**, you can use this file in your project by replacing the old **bootstrap.css** (we will discuss how to compile a Less file in the following section). Henceforth, whenever you use the modal component it will use the customized style. In Figure 5.4 is a screenshot showing the customized modal component.

Figure 5.4. Modal customized with Less

Compiling Less

Compiling Less is relatively straightforward. Here, I am going to show you some of the standard ways of doing it.

Using Node

If you have Node installed, you can use Node's package manager to install the `less` compiler:

```
$ npm install -g less
```

Once `less` is installed, use the following command to compile **bootstrap.less** into **bootstrap.css**. You have to navigate to the **/less** folder using the command prompt and then type this command:

```
$ lessc bootstrap.less > bootstrap.css
```

Using Third-party Software

There are plenty of GUI applications for writing and compiling Less code. Some of the popular options include Crunch![3], SimpLESS,[4] and Mixture.[5]

Customizing Bootstrap before Downloading

Yes, you heard right. Bootstrap allows you to edit and select the features you want that should be present inside your own custom Bootstrap package.[6]

It has a field beside each Less variable, so if you don't know how to use Less you can use this form to edit the default values. It also has a checkbox alongside each Bootstrap component and plugin. You can uncheck any that you don't want to use, as shown in Figure 5.5.

---

[3] http://crunchapp.net/
[4] http://wearekiss.com/simpless
[5] http://mixture.io/
[6] http://getbootstrap.com/customize

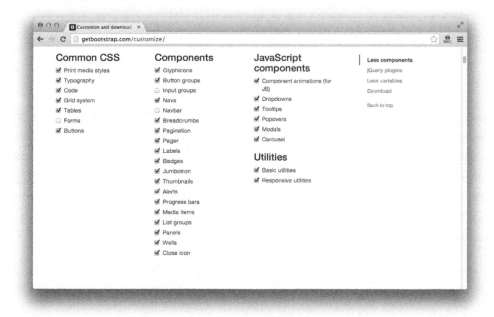

Figure 5.5. Customizing the Bootstrap package

Unchecking a particular component may also uncheck other components that are dependent on it. For example, unchecking `Forms` from the customize page will also uncheck `Input groups` and `Navbar` automatically. Hence, you need to be careful when making selections!

Media Queries and Bootstrap

Media queries were introduced as a part of CSS3 to dynamically control website content depending on screen resolution. It's one of the key technologies beneath every responsive framework available today. Bootstrap uses media queries to properly define many CSS rules to make it a responsive framework.

Understanding media queries is important if you want to customize Bootstrap's responsive grid system. Let's take a look at a simple media query:

```
@media all and (min-width: 699px){
    h1{
        display: none;
    }
}
```

Every media query should have a media type and an expression. The **media type** specifies on what type of devices the linked document will be displayed Here, the media type is `all`. The **expression** further limits the stylesheet's scope using **media features**, such as width, height, and color. Here, the expression is `min-width: 699px`. This media query will apply the CSS properties contained in it if the browser width is greater than 699px. Hence, the `h1` element will be hidden on screens wider than 699px.

There are many media types and media features available to us. Examples of media types include `all`, `print`, `screen`, and `projection`. Examples of media features include `height`, `max-height`, and `max-width`.

Bootstrap has defined many media queries for various device sizes to create a highly responsive framework. One of the snippets from Bootstrap's CSS file is shown here:

```
@media (min-width: 768px) {
    .container {
        width: 750px;
    }
}
```

To read more about media queries, refer to the Mozilla Developer Network documentation.[7]

Summary

In this chapter, we've discussed the various ways of customizing Bootstrap and seen how to customize Bootstrap via CSS and Less. As we've seen, Bootstrap offers many options for altering the default styles, giving you the power to create your own unique and beautiful designs.

---

[7] https://developer.mozilla.org/en-US/docs/Web/Guide/CSS/Media_queries

Optimizing Bootstrap

So we have reached the final chapter of the book. We've really come a long way, now having the capability to build a professional, responsive website using Bootstrap. But the final piece of the puzzle is discovering how to optimize our creations so that they not only look good but also perform well.

In this chapter, you will be learning techniques to optimize a website built with Bootstrap (or, indeed, any other front-end framework). We will be working with CSS and JavaScript minification and also streamlining the Bootstrap default package. We will try to understand the limitations of Bootstrap and discuss some of the common pitfalls of using it.

Optimization Techniques

A website needs to look good and perform well. Web users have become impatient, and a slow-loading website will be dismissed, irrespective of how beautifully designed it is.

In order to build the right template, we need to optimize our CSS files, JavaScript files, and images. All these files are served to the browser via separate request calls, so the lighter they are, the better the overall performance of the website.

Optimizing CSS

When dealing with the Bootstrap framework, we generally end up creating more than one CSS file. By default, every Bootstrap project comes with the **bootstrap.css** file included in the website's template. On top of that, we will normally have custom CSS files to make our website look more attractive. Here are a few tasks we can do to reduce the size of the CSS files in our website's template.

Use the Minified Bootstrap CSS File

As stated in the previous chapter, Bootstrap allows developers to select only those components that are actually needed while developing the template. This reduces the overall size of the main Bootstrap CSS file (**bootstrap.css**). Once the website is ready for production, we can further reduce the size of this CSS file by using its minified version (**bootstrap.min.css**).

Remove Unused Bootstrap Components Using Less

If you prefer writing CSS through Less, you have the additional option of customizing Bootstrap through its main Less file (**bootstrap.less**). If you open this file, you'll see lots of import statements aggregating various Bootstrap components together. You can comment out those import statements that are irrelevant to your template.

For example, to avoid using Bootstrap's labels, badges, and progress bars, you can comment out the following lines from **bootstrap.less** file:

```
@import "labels.less";
@import "badges.less";
@import "progress-bars.less";
```

Suppose that you don't want to use any of Bootstrap's JavaScript plugins. Remove all the CSS rules associated with them by commenting out the following lines from **bootstrap.less** to exclude them completely:

```
// Components w/ JavaScript
@import "modals.less";
@import "tooltip.less";
@import "popovers.less";
@import "carousel.less";
```

You can also remove the default font icons (glyphicons) that are built into the Bootstrap package. First you need to delete all the glyphicon-* font files from the **fonts** folder. Then comment out the following import statement from **bootstrap.less** file:

```
@import "glyphicons.less";
```

After you're done commenting out those components that you won't be using, compile the main **bootstrap.less** file to form **bootstrap.css**, as discussed in the previous chapter. This way you can reduce the size of the CSS file.

Compress all the CSS Files into One File

After developing your website's template, you will likely be left with a version of Bootstrap's CSS file and multiple custom CSS files. You can combine all these files into one CSS file, which will help in reducing the number of HTTP requests, as well as the combined size of all the CSS files.

There are several tools to help you with the compression process. One of my favorites is Recess from Twitter,[1] an open-source code quality tool for CSS. You can read how to install and use Recess at SitePoint.[2]

Let's first combine all the CSS files into a main one called **application.css**. This can done using CSS's @import statement as follows:

---

[1] http://twitter.github.io/recess/
[2] ttp://www.sitepoint.com/optimizing-css-stylesheets-recess/

```
@import url("bootstrap.min.css");
@import url("myCSSFile1.css");
@import url("myCSSFile2.css");
@import url("myCSSFile3.css");
@import url("myCSSFile4.css");
```

You need to ensure that you are providing relative paths in the import statements with respect to **application.css**.

Next, run the `recess` command in the terminal:

```
recess path/to/application.css --compress >
➥path/to/application.min.css
```

This will create a new CSS file called **application.min.css** in the same folder. This new CSS file will be much smaller in size than the original separate files.

Optimizing JavaScript

Optimizing the JavaScript files is equally as important as optimizing the CSS files. Bootstrap comes with flexible options to remove any unwanted JavaScript plugins that we won't be using in our projects. This can greatly help in reducing the size of the main JavaScript file **bootstrap.js**.

Use a Minified Bootstrap JavaScript file

If you want to be able to use all of Bootstrap's JavaScript plugins, you should include the minified file **bootstrap.min.js** file rather than **bootstrap.js** when sending the project for production.

Remove Unused Bootstrap JavaScript plugins

Just like we did for CSS components, you can head over to Bootstrap's customization page and deselect any JavaScript plugins you don't need before downloading. This can be the easiest way of removing unwanted JavaScript plugins from Bootstrap.

Bootstrap also comes with a separate `.js` file for each of its JavaScript plugins. For example, it has **modal.js** for modals and **carousel.js** for carousels. You can access these individual files only if you have downloaded Bootstrap's source package.

Going to the Source Package

Bootstrap's source package can be obtained by selecting the **Download Source** option at the Bootstrap download page.[3]

Once downloaded, you can head over to the **js** folder to find all the **.js** files related to each of Bootstrap's JavaScript plugins. You can then include just those files in your project that you want to use.

Compress All the JavaScript Files into One

Just as with CSS, it is a good idea to have all your JavaScript files compressed into a single .js file. One of my favorite JavaScript compression tools is CompressJS, which is found on its GitHub page to download the package.[4] With CompressJS, you have to provide the paths to all the **.js** files with a space between them.

Here's an example:

```
$ ./compressjs.sh jquery.min.js bootstrap.min.js
➥myCustomJavaScript.js
```

This command will compile all the JavaScript files and produce the output in a single .js file. It gives a random name to the compressed file and tells you the file-name. If you have many JavaScript files, you can place them all in a single folder and compile them together as follows:

```
$ ./compressjs.sh scripts/*.js
```

The terminal output should be similar to Figure 6.1.

---

[3] http://getbootstrap.com/getting-started/#download
[4] https://github.com/dfsq/compressJS.sh

Figure 6.1. Running CompressJS

Optimizing Images

It is often the images that cause the slow loading of web pages. Imagine a situation where we need to display an image of resolution 500px by 500px but instead we have an image of resolution 2000px by 2000px. We can use Bootstrap's helper class `img-responsive` to fit that bigger image into a 500px by 500px div; however, while the helper class has assisted in displaying the image properly, it hasn't actually reduced the file size of the image. Unfortunately, Bootstrap lacks the tools to fix this issue.

There are several server-side tools that can identify the request type of a particular image and then resize the image before serving it. Some of the tools I've been using are Adaptive Images[5] and TimThumb,[6] but I won't be covering them in this book as they are server-side tools. Installation and usage instructions are available on their official websites.

---

[5] http://adaptive-images.com/
[6] http://www.binarymoon.co.uk/projects/timthumb/

Avoiding Common Pitfalls

By now, you'll understand that Bootstrap is one of the best frameworks for building responsive websites. With Bootstrap, there's no need to develop a separate mobile version of your site. A single responsive version can be viewed on any kind of device.

Yet there are a few common pitfalls that Bootstrap developers often fall into while developing responsive websites. These issues can make your websites slow and non-responsive in smaller devices, so be aware of them:

- **Using different HTML markup for specific devices**: New developers often take advantage of Bootstrap's responsive utility features such as `hidden-sm` and `visible-sm` to toggle the display of various components on a website. They write different versions of the HTML markup in one document and then use these helper classes to toggle the component display as per the browser window size. By doing this they forget that the overall size of the HTML page is increasing, which will slow down the rendering process. Hence, it is advisable to use Bootstrap's grid system to dynamically resize the same HTML markup in browsers of all sizes.

- **Using Bootstrap in applications that target IE8 and below:** I have seen larger organizations that still target compatibility with Internet Explorer version 8 and below. Though Bootstrap does provide support for IE8, there are some CSS3 properties that will fail to work in it such as `border-radius` and `box-shadows`. Therefore it is advisable to avoid using Bootstrap if your target audience is IE8 and lower. In fact, you definitely should not use Bootstrap 3 in applications that target audiences with IE7 and below.

- **Using Bootstrap to make hybrid mobile applications**: You should avoid using Bootstrap to create hybrid applications that are developed using web-based technologies and then ported into mobile platforms. Bootstrap can be too heavy for such applications. You can instead use the Ratchet framework,[7] which is developed especially for creating mobile applications. Ratchet comes from the same Bootstrap team, and you can learn more about it on SitePoint.[8]

---

[7] http://goratchet.com
[8] http://www.sitepoint.com/prototype-mobile-apps-easily-ratchet/

The Bootstrap team keeps on releasing newer versions by fixing known problems and adding new features. You can also check out Bootstrap's official issues page to keep track of current known issues with Bootstrap 3.[9]

Where to Go From Here

As the saying goes, "practice makes perfect." The more you practice with Bootstrap, the better control you have on your designs. One way to practice is to try to recreate the designs of popular responsive websites using Bootstrap. Here's a list of websites you can take inspiration from:

- Hudson's Bay Company[10]
- Dribbble[11]
- Google+[12]
- Pinterest[13]
- Zurb[14]
- Sony[15]
- Microsoft[16]
- Bootstrap[17]

We've taken a look at some built-in Bootstrap plugins in this book, but it's also worth investigating some of the third-party Bootstrap plugins that are available as they can add powerful features to your sites. Here's a selection of the most popular:

- FuelUX[18] adds various popular features such as datepicker, checkbox, combobox, loader, pill box, and tree.

---

[9] https://github.com/twbs/bootstrap/issues

[10] http://www3.hbc.com/

[11] http://dribbble.com/

[12] http://plus.google.com

[13] http://www.pinterest.com

[14] http://www.zurb.com

[15] http://www.sony.com

[16] http://www.microsoft.com

[17] http://getbootstrap.com

[18] https://github.com/ExactTarget/fuelux/tree/3.0.0-wip

- Jasny Bootstrap[19] brings in some important features that were not available in Bootstrap 3. For example, off canvas (a slide-out menu from either side of the screen like in apps for mobile devices), row link (converting table rows into clickable links), input mask (forcing user to enter data in a specific format), and file input (a stylish file input field).

- Bootstrap Lightbox[20] adds an image lightbox feature to Bootstrap.

- Bootstrap Image Gallery[21] comes with a fully functional, ready-to-use image gallery for Bootstrap.

- Bootstrap Notifications[22] gives the capability to display fancy notifications anywhere on the screen.

- Bootstrap Markdown[23] provides markdown editing tools in Bootstrap.

- Bootstrap Colorpicker[24] adds a color-picker widget.

- Bootstrap Star Rating[25] provides star rating tools.

You should try out Bootstrap in your upcoming projects to get a feel for the rapid development environment that it promises. You can also follow the Bootstrap tutorials on SitePoint to explore more. Keep Bootstrapping!

---

[19] http://jasny.github.io/bootstrap/

[20] http://www.jasonbutz.info/bootstrap-lightbox/

[21] http://blueimp.github.io/Bootstrap-Image-Gallery/)

[22] http://goodybag.github.io/bootstrap-notify/

[23] http://toopay.github.io/bootstrap-markdown/

[24] http://www.eyecon.ro/bootstrap-colorpicker/

[25] http://plugins.krajee.com/star-rating

CPSIA information can be obtained
at www.ICGtesting.com
Printed in the USA
BVOW11s1132230817

492887BV00010B/57/P